Liberation and Domestication

YOUNG PEOPLE, YOUTH POLICY and CULTURAL
CREATIVITY

John Astley

The COMPANY *of* WRITERS
2005

First Published in the United Kingdom 2005
by The Company of Writers
www.thecompanyofwriters.com

© 2005 John Astley

John Astley has asserted his right under the Copyright,
Designs and Patents Act 1988.

Paperback
ISBN: 0-9551834-0-5
& ISBN: 978-0-9551834-0-9

Set in Book Antiqua   305.235
                          AST

British Library Cataloguing in Publication Data.
A catalogue record for this book is available from the British Library.

Classification: Non-Fiction
Social Sciences/Culture/Contemporary Society (UK)/
Youth Policy

BIC Codes
J/JB/JBMP2

Bibliographic Data also available:
Nielsen Book Data

Acknowledgements

I am grateful to the National Youth Agency for permission to print 'Youth Policy Making in the 1950s', and to Philip Allan for permission to reprint 'Present Imperfect: Future Tense' and 'Seen but not Heard', both from *Sociology Review*.

Steve Nyman has also given his agreement to our joint piece being published.

A thank you also to Wendy for doing the typing.

This book is to dedicated to my parents, Violet and Harry, the kind of parents that every young person would be fortunate to have had.

CONTENTS

INTRODUCTION

The essays collected together here represent my thinking on these issues over some time. One reason for choosing to publish this selection now is to make them more widely available in one piece rather then the endless photocopying, referring people to journals, and so on.

There are a few uniting themes here that it is worth my outlining and briefly reflecting upon.

A good deal of what is said in these essays is concerned with the oppression which young people in general experience in contemporary Britain. This is not to suggest that young people are unique in this respect, and the pervasive impact of the relationships of capitalism, and cultural elitism, is there for all to behold. Britain is still a society greatly affected by the reasons for the creation, and everyday maintenance, of social classes. Why, how, and in what form this happens, are questions that, for a sociologist like myself, are never far away. Nor should they be, because despite the appearances of contemporary life, portrayed for example through the myth making apparatuses of media, advertising, and party politics, inequalities of power, status, opportunity, and life chances are rife.

Those of us explicitly working for, and with young people, are confronted daily with the nature and consequences of this fundamental unfairness and lack of social justice. In our attempts to empower young people, to ensure that they have a voice to participate in decisions that affect them (and others in their communities), battles with negativity and adultism are commonplace.

As the reader will discover, these essays also deal with concerns about the creation of ideas, images, and values, and the way these interrelated private and public domains are central to our everyday cultures. As with all discussions about culture, it is important here to emphasise the relationships between continuity and change. We must keep asking ourselves why there is cultural continuity *here*, and change *there*? And from a fundamental sociological perspective this raises structure and agency issues. How do certain characeristics, social structures, and in institutional forms - like family and schooling - have a bearing on the lives of young people? In what form are these structures the everyday contexts to life and living? This in turn requires us to question the extent and nature of agency that young people have available to them. There are inevitably issues here around both structural aspects of power, those contexts again, and the day-to-day situational manifestations of these inequalities of power and status (for example, in the schooling system).

Young people, like the rest of us, do take action in both thought and deed; however, that action-taking is not necessarily in conditions of their own choosing.

The Blair government, as with all such regimes based on neo-liberal ideologies, like to make a lot of the nature and role of choice. They (the regime) have quite frequently been reminded that what constitutes the range of choices available to people in general, and the young in particular, are circumscribed, and even compromised, by the realities of everyday life within a consumer-oriented capitalism. One area of debate has focused on the so-called 'post code lottery' of access to welfare provisions, services and the like. And, of course, locality is an important issue, but it remains only one influential factor alongside the other persistent, potentially discriminating, and disadvantaging features of society. Social class, gender, and ethnicity still play a major role in the lives of young people, acting as enabling, and disabling forces in turn. We are not short of information on the severe limitations to social mobility in the UK.

The constant rubbishing of 'comprehensive' education reflects the Labour hierarchy's determination to turn away from egalitarian ideals, and place even more emphasis on the notion of meritocracy. But attempts to raise expectations among young people, and their families, have foundered on the social and economic realities of the last thirty years. Reflecting on the Labour leaderships' (why am I so reluctant to use that phrase?) 1970s' decision to abandon the social demoatic commitment to the 'post war settlement' and a public sector led welfare state, Tony Crosland famously commented that, "the party is over". The trouble is, who has been left behind after the party to clean up the mess?

In addition to this, we do not lack evidence that suggests that the already privileged in society have many opportunities to maintain, and even enhance their position in the hierarchy. The neo-liberals across the party political spectrum make a great deal of their schemes to provide access to some bastion of privilege, like independent schools, that might provide a leg-up for some child. They might as well introduce an 'emptying the ocean with a spoon' policy as well!

Another theme in these essays concerns the role of cultural creativity in the lives of young people.

The essay 'Being an Agent of Change' focuses on this issue, and draws on the admirable work of Paul Willis. In the essays that follow this one I have tried to map out ideas that emphasise the value of cultural creativity to young people, and wider society. The human labour that young people expend on a vast array of creative activities serves several purposes for them individually and collectively, and, as I argue, might be seen as (at least in part) an antidote to the alienating tendencies in their everyday lives. This is why, for example, and to paraphrase Stuart Hall, these creative actions are the 'sites of struggle'. The 'pick and mix' approach to so much youthful creativity serves to emphasise the realities of living amongst cultural diversity, and a desire to be open and innovative in both personal and public domains.

Here is a daily demonstration of a genuine internationalism that should make ethnocentrics in the UK truly ashamed of their negativity and lack of vision. The piece co-written with Steve Nyman looks at another long-standing concern. Indeed, I am sad to report that my experience with such matters has not changed much over the intervening years. Feeling uneasy about the values, thought processes and everyday actions of low-level bureaucrats cannot be unique to Nyman and myself. I still regularly encounter the role holder whose sole aim in (their working) life seems to be the maintenance of the organisation that provides them with a relatively comfortable living. All too often in my experience such role holders rarely reflect upon the basic fact that their job exists because the client(s) exist. Of course the organisation and role holders may operate at the behest of a State that is much more interested in control rather than care, where clients are seen as a set of problems to be managed. It is all too easy for practitioners to fall in with this way of thinking about the welfare needs of young people, and the oppressive and inflexible regimes that can often result. The very idea of young people having an independent and equal voice in decision-making processes about their own lives (at the very least) is anathema to many officials of a diverse kind.

So, liberation and domestication for young people? An enlightened freedom, with genuine choices, and scope for autonomy and independence? Or, more controls, pressures to fit in regardless of conflicts around values, and to continue to be subservient to the dominating elites in their everyday lives? The history of reforms to meet the needs of young people demonstrates the uneven processes of both change and continuity. Two steps forward and one step back in policy and practice is probably being optimistic most of the time, but we can strive for at least that.

In view of the nature of essay writing over time, and related to the specific circumstances of that writing, the reader will note some inevitable minor repetitions. These reflect the cumulative nature of my thinking, and I trust I might be excused on this occasion? I have also resisted the temptation to revise these essays, despite the fact that I might not choose to say things in exactly the same way now. They were meant then, so they should stand or fall on their contemporary merits.

As is always the case, I encourage discussion and debate, and would welcome responses to what is to be found in these pages.

John Astley
Exmouth, 2005

Present imperfect: future tense?

1990

YOUTH POLICY IN THE 1990s

Young people are often in the news, but not always for the best of reasons. The 'anti-social' or 'self-destructive' activities of youth, although involving a very small minority, attract sensational headlines. The media attention given to the apparently chronic problems of some young people, *e.g.*, unemployment or home-lessness, accentuates certain aspects of the dependence and vulnerability felt by many teenagers and young adults.

These issues and 'media events' certainly do contribute to a widespread belief amongst many sections of society that a comprehensive set of 'youth' policies are both necessary and desirable.

The opening of a new decade is a particularly interesting time to assess the nature of policy focused on the future and the social changes that recent policy has created. This is certainly so with a study of Youth Policy at a time when so many changes are on the agenda but within a context of debates about the British Welfare State and Inter-generational relations, that has changed very little for decades (Wicks, 1987: Cole, 1986).

Sociologists often argue that social policy is one of the clearest demonstrations by the powerful in society of the kind of life they would like people to be leading now and in the future. It is also very evident that most sociological analysis, which may seek to influence social policy, is rooted in an examination and understanding of the recent past.

THE DEMOGRAPHIC TIMEBOMB

One way in which young people in the UK have hit the headlines recently is with regard to just how few teenagers there are compared with other post-war decades. 16-19 year-olds have been the main focus of attention because they are at their lowest numbers in the population for some time. In the first half of the 1990s, the number of 16-24 year-olds will fall by about 1.2 million. Over the same period, the number of 16-19 year-olds in the British workforce will fall by some 23% - from 2.5 million to 1.9 million. This is the school-leaving seeking work or training or further education and adult status, freedom and independence group par excellence. Not surprisingly, therefore, this cohort is being watched carefully, intensively researched, speculated about, and is generally at the centre of continued political and media scrutiny (Bynner, 1987: Roberts, 1987: Courtenay, 1988).

THE 1980s, THE DECADE OF CONTINUED CONTRADICTIONS FOR YOUTH

The 1980s have been dubbed the decade of appearances, the years when superficial symbols of status and success replaced real progress and substance in people's lives. If we are to understand Youth Policy for the 1990s, what can the policies and their implementation in the 1980s tell us? This was the decade of 'Thatcherism', of the Enterprise Culture, of YUPPIES and fast money. It was the decade of increasing evidence of the multi-cultural reality of British society evidenced through phenomena as diverse as pop music and personal fashion styles to urban riots and the reaction to it. Young people in a refashioned multi-cultural context continued to dominate the headlines but not always in very sympathetic ways. Young people dubbed as deviant for one reason or another (*e.g.*, football hooliganism and vagrancy) certainly continued to be a focus for policy shapers and policy makers, but invariably, in a time-honoured way, as social problems. Policy was certainly needed for youth, but these policies were usually couched in a negative way related to some problem which needed 'to be nipped in the bud' rather than in a positive way to seek the co-operation of young people in shaping Britain's future (Muncie, 1984: Davies, 1986).

Those practitioners directly associated with the young came to see the '80s as a decade when many young were increasingly under pressure and at risk (Skinner, 1988: Jeffs and Smith, 1987).

YOUTH POLICY AND SOCIAL CONTROL

One of the consistent themes in sociological analysis of youth policy has been the debate around social (and by definition, personal) control. What is compulsory schooling for? Why insist that unemployed school-leavers take a YTS course? Why deprive 16 and 17 year-olds of access to Income Support, or change the Board and Lodging rules for under 25s, thus condemning substantial numbers of young people to an increased dependency on their families? Why continue to spend far more money on measures aimed at juvenile delinquents than is spent on recreational and other youth services? Are these measures part of a strategy by Government to keep young people dependent, powerless, frustrated and under control? Sociologists in Britain as elsewhere have argued that most Youth orientated policy seems to be about keeping the young 'in their place' rather than liberating them to a status of equal partners in society. It is certainly true that many, probably most, people working with youth in Britain today - youth and community workers, social workers, teachers, voluntary work organisers, *etc.* - are striving to open up new and better horizons for the younger generation. However, it could be argued that their efforts have been set against a background where government has been mainly concerned to use its considerable powers to exercise continued social control over 'threatening youth' (Bates, 1984: Pitts, 1988: Lee, 1990).

One of the key debates amongst sociologists has been focused on the culturally creative activities of young people. The mass media remain a significant influence in all our lives. Young people do tend to be self-conscious inter-actors with different media, especially those clustered around pop cultures. It is certainly true that these media forms both absorb a great deal of leisure time and inspire young people to develop 'their own' culture responses. But how much manipulation by commercial interests and via dominant ideologies goes on? Debate has invariably focused on whether the young can really be liberated by their fashion-conscious engagement in media and pop cultures or whether these uses form a further constraining and controlling, 'domesticating' youth? (Tomlinson, 1990).

YOUNG PEOPLE AND ADULT STATUS

It is quite clear that most children and young people spend an enormous amount of time both in and out of school, training, work, *etc.*, preparing themselves for adulthood. This is not even peculiar to advanced industrial societies like Britain. All human societies appear to have endless debates about what constitutes proper adult role performance and the socialisation processes that will take the young into these highly valued statuses (O'Donnell, 1985: Brake, 1985: Beloff, 1986). However, given the increasing diversity of societies like Britain these debates about adult roles have become increasingly problematic, even tortuous! Societies like ours do quite unashamedly use whatever social policies can be devised to determine the passage of young people into adult roles. One dimension of the sociological debates in recent years has, under-standably, focused upon the question of social and cultural differences among the young. There was a time in the 1960s when some people suggested that young people were all the same, a homogeneous group culturally. That is no more true today than it was then and an increasing amount of research and analysis has been devoted to class, gender and racial differences amongst the young (McRobbie, 1984: Cockburn, 1987: Cohen, 1988). It may be the case that the powerful in society, those individuals and groups that do have access to policy making, feel that progression to adult status of a certain kind is going to be a more straightforward and acceptable process for some young people than for others. There are many influences on young people's expectations in modern Britain and many of these influences may be difficult for the government or others to control. It is ironic perhaps that in recent years, government has promoted the influence of commercial interests in the 'market place' over those of the public sector. However, these moves can only heighten the familiar concerns that adults have continued to have about undesirable influences over the young (Astley, 1987: Cohen, 1980). Popular cultures have in particular been identified as 'sites of struggle' where those with power have sought to maintain their moral authority over the ideas and behaviour of the young. This ideological and hegemonic struggle is not new but recent sociological debates have increasingly focused on the contra-dictions for young people living and growing up in Britain (Hall and Jefferson, 1976: Pearson, 1983: Mungham and Pearson, 1976: Robins and Cohen, 1978: Willis, 1977: Coffied, 1986). Most of this research evidence has suggested that most young people fall victim to well organised schemes to persuade them to accept ideas, take on certain kinds of knowledge, and behave in ways that reproduce social and power relations very much as they are. Maintenance of the social and cultural status quo appears to be a high priority amongst the older generation. Set against this rather pessimistic account is the vibrant symbolic creativity of young people in particular. Each new generation devises cultural means by which to have their say, to resist domination, to be creative and take a part in shaping their lives and the world today and in the future (Willis, 1978: Hebdige, 1979: Astley, 1981: Frith, 1983, Willis, 1990).

PREPARING YOUNG PEOPLE TO BE GOOD
AND ACTIVE CITIZENS

The government is at this time intending to rationalise its funding of the national youth service agencies. From April 1991, a number of existing national agencies, which are concerned with Youth Policy and the training of Youth workers, *etc.*, are to be merged. (The National Youth Bureau and The Council for Education and Training in Youth and Community Work are the most significant.)

The voluntary sector, with many long standing organisations focused on youth, looks set to play an even greater role in the lives of young people in Britain. Services for youth are no exception in post-war Britain where the voluntary sector has played a considerable part. Recent moves by some influential persons have, however, increased interest in the role of voluntary work for young people as a character building, adult role modelling exercise. HRH the Prince of Wales has now formally launched his national 'Volunteer' corps. He has been developing his ideas on young volunteers for many years now. Perhaps his father's award scheme was an influence on him? The Prince has suggested in the past that young people would benefit from a form active community-based service, by way of "compulsory-volunteering", to last for two years. This idea has found much favour in a society that has not had compulsory National Armed Forces service since the 1950s. This is not to say that young people do not or would not benefit from 'serving the community' or deny the possible value for society as a whole of much more specific focus on the best way for young people to become good adults and model citizens. Unfortunately, these policies, or their spokespersons, do not usually address questions of *whose* values are to be counted as important and who will continue to make key decisions. This may leave some sceptical people wondering, Is the motive behind some apparently well-intentioned ideas more social control? (Astley, 1989).

In addition to these issues is the contradiction created by the 'Poll Tax' in that many young people will not register for the community charge and fail to be on a voters list as a consequence. As mentioned elsewhere in this article, many young people have experienced a significant decline in their standard of living through changes in social security regulations and housing benefit, cuts in training grants, cutbacks in students loans, *etc., etc.*

On the one hand young people are getting the message to feel part of a caring, sharing society, while at the same time being denied the basic resources to lead a decent life, be independent and have some self-respect!

YOUTH POLICY AND PARTY POLITICAL POLICY

Within the next two years there will be a general election. All of the political parties are preparing their campaigns and devoting considerable time and money to the formation of manifestos. The aims of these parties will be spelt out over the next year and it will be very interesting to see just how much, or little, these prospective governments actually say about youth policy. At least one political party has to my knowledge engaged in some debate about co-ordinated and comprehensive youth policy for the future. The aim of those involved in providing advice has certainly been to draw on social scientific theory and research evidence to propose and draft policy recommendations. Those proposals aim to develop a context for the development of comprehensive policies that will improve the standard of living and quality of life of young people and create a policy-making framework that enables young people to have much more say over the shaping of society as a whole. Giving young people more power, more say, to actually make choices is a key feature of most progressive-looking policy and practice. However, as I

23

have suggested above, this is not easy given the usual mistrust of most young people by those already in power. In addition, it is important to remind ourselves that an analysis of the condition of youth in Britain today, and prospects for the future, is also a class, gender and race issue. Young people in modern Britain are not (and never have been) a homogeneous grouping. There are considerable, crucial, cultural differences amongst the 'young generation' and within any development of coherent policies to raise the standard of living and decision-making opportunities of the young, special attention has to be given to these significant inequalities 'within' youth.

REFERENCES:

ASTLEY, J. *'Youth service policy making in the 1950s'*, Youth and Policy, No. 19,. 1987.

ASTLEY, J. *Youth Policy: A Collection of Readings and Sources*, Oxford Polytechnic, 1989

BATES, I., *et al. Schooling for the Dole, The New Vocationalism*, Macmillan, 1984 .

BRAKE, M. *Comparative Youth Culture*, RKP, 1985

COFFIELD, F., Borrill, C. and Marshall, S. *Growing up at the Margins*, Open University Press, 1986.

COHEN, P. and Brains, H. (Ed's.), *Multi-racist Britain*, Macmillan, 1988.

COHEN, S. *Folk Devils and Moral Panics*, Martin Robertson, 1980

DAVIES, B. *Threatening Youth: Towards a National Youth Policy*, Open University Press, 1986

FRITH, S. *Sound Effects. Youth, Leisure and the Politics of Rock*, Constable, 1983

LEE, D. *et al. Scheming for Youth: A Study of YTS in the Enterprise Culture*, Open University Press, 1990.

McROBBIE, A. and Nava, N. (Ed's). *Gender and Generation*,

MacMillan, 1984.

MUNCIE, J. *'The trouble with kids today', Youth and Crime in Postwar Britain*, Hutchinson, 1984.

SKINNER, A.L. *Young People under Pressure: a Statistical Report*, National Youth Bureau, 1988.

TOMLINSON, A. (Ed.). *Consumption, Identity and Style*, Comedia, 1990

WILLIS, P. *Common Culture*, Open University Press, 1990.

Seen, but not heard: the situation of young people in contemporary Britain
2004

NEW LEGISLATION

The new Children Bill has the clear aim of protecting children and meeting their welfare needs, seeking to set in place adequate organisational means whereby these aims can be met at a local level. It should be noted that this Bill, like the Green Paper, 'Every Child Matters' (2003) that preceded it, is actually about young people as well! Older teenagers do not actually feature very much in this legislation and what I would like to do in this article is set out a sociological explanation for this striking omission. However, whatever such legislation may be called the practical implications, for the everyday lives of children and young people and their families, are significant. It should also be noted that many professionals working in a diverse range of welfare provision - care, services and benefits - have great empathy with young people and strive to meet their needs.

WELFARE RIGHTS

Young people have welfare needs and they also already have a set of rights that give them access to provisions to meet those needs. For example, the UK Government has, since 1991, been a signatory to the United Nations Convention on the Rights of the Child (UNCRC). The provisions of this rights charter can be summed up in the 3Ps, protection, provision and participation. It is with the key issue of participation that I would like to concentrate. Do young people have a 'voice' and a clear role in the diverse range of discussions that contribute to decisions made about their everyday lives and futures? One of the initiatives currently taken by those working with young people is empowerment. What this approach acknowledges is that there is an inequality in power that is manifest in the relationships between most young people and most older people. The process of empowerment seeks to redress this imbalance by, for example, raising young people's expectations, providing access to resources, and encouraging them to engage in decision making individually and, where appropriate, collectively. It has to be said that despite some positive changes in inter-generational relationships there is still considerable resistance to these ideas of equity and social justice. So why is this?

A good deal of policy that gives structure to and influences the lives of young people feeds on the negative stereotypes about 'youth' that are always with us. In certain sections of the media, national and local, there is usually something sensational and derogatory to say about young people's values and behaviour. By using the catchall term 'youth', young people are seen as a homogeneous group culturally and consistently problematised, if not criminalised. The Government's enthusiasm for 'anti-social behaviour' legislation and increased use of incarceration are examples of reactions and responses to media led public opinion.

NEGATIVE STEREOTYPES

Christine Griffin (1993), in her social constructivist approach, suggests that this problematisation rests on the 3Ds view of young people, dysfunction: deficit and deviance. The young are not socialised and socially controlled adequately, they do not achieve enough educationally and they are often rule breakers. I suggested as much in an article ("Present Imperfect: Future Tense?") that appeared in the first issue of *Sociology Review* in 1991. I argued there that policy about young people is consistently of the care and control type and that successive UK governments use age-specific criteria to inform policy that keeps young people in their place, in a state of dependency. For example, as post-16 education has expanded, fuelled by expectations of a good job and better life, more young people have been schooled in the costs of extending their 'childhood' dependency.

TRANSITIONS

One important focus of social policy with regard to young people is that of transition. I was young once, but (alas) I had to grow up, no Peter Pan existence for me! In making policy, governments realise that they need to shape young people's aspirations and expectations. The young have to be prepared for the reality of adult roles, particularly work roles. Work role socialisation remains a key aspect of social policy from the increasing emphasis on an employer-focused skills base in the curriculum, to the ever-present recognition that many young people are disaffected, and disengaged from the main agencies of work role socialisation. A good deal of money and effort has been poured into New Deal and, more recently, into Connexions. The former policy was linked with New Labour concerns with the consequences of social exclusion, an aspect of their 'welfare to work' ideology. Connexions was heralded as a universal guidance service for all teenagers and although often in reality targeted at young people with 'special problems', has met with a degree of success (*see, for example,* 'Transforming Youth Work' (2001) *and the regular updates in* 'zero2nineteen'). However, sociological research has shown that the vagaries of a market economy, stark local variations, for example in the costs of industrial change and the continued ideological dominance of neo-liberalism, create un-certainty and risk in the lives of the young.

So young people are exhorted to be choice makers, to have 'adult' aspirations and tastes, but, for most, without the means to realise them.

AGE STRATIFICATION AND POLICY

The particular significance of transitions from pre- to post-16 education, to training, to work and so on, is very much a concern of policy makers and the vast diversity of practitioners working with young people. These age-related 'stages' have to be managed in order to achieve desired outcomes. Who sets the agenda for

most of these transition-related interventions into the lives of young people is another matter of course! One key issue here is that the neo-liberal emphasis in policy continues to argue for individual solutions to social problems. What proposals there are for community based solutions to the arbitrariness of life within a set of socio-economic relations dominated by capitalism tend to be short-term funded and invariably undemocratic (*see* REFERENCES - 'findings').

Phil Mizen makes a similar point in his book *The Changing State of Youth* (2004), where he suggests that policy can be seen as a set of strategies to (re)integrate young people into a contradictory set of relations dominated by capitalism. The dominant values of conformity to established and institutionalised authority and the centrality of status derived from working and consuming are ever present.

Our membership of age specific groups is an important fact of life for most of us. This can be very relevant say in the lives of the elderly in British society. Our membership of these 'age-related' socio-cultural groups emphasises the role of our peers as a reference point for our values and behaviour. It may be that membership of such an age-specific group is the most influential aspect of our everyday lives and the meanings we place upon our experiences are mediated through that group. To what extent is our sense of self, our self-identity, developed within and derived from such 'membership'?

YOUNG PEOPLE, CULTURE AND POWER

As sociologists we understand that culture, our values within everyday ways of life, is a process that embraces some key features:

People's conventional social relationships;
The symbolic forms available to them for focusing on and co-ordinating experience;
Their systems of belief, values and motives for action.

Paul Willis (1990) has used the concept *grounded aesthetics* to suggest that young people do have ownership of a worked-through cultural basis to their ideas and behaviour. These *lived* processes often have an element of resistance to oppression and new - soundings creative innovation about them. This action taking is invariably seen as a threat to establishment cultural values, or fair game to be 'colonised', commercialised, packaged, branded and sold back to young people. Not surprisingly, then, the 'grass roots' cultures of young people are what Stuart Hall (1976) has called 'sites of struggle'. There are many aspects of hegemonic struggle to consider here. Maria Pini (2004), in drawing on the ideas of Foucault (1976), has made similar comments on the use young people make of their bodies and the attempts by others to 'manage' our body. Pini argues that our sense of self is portrayed through the way in which our body is disciplined, classified and so on by our self and/or by others. Our bodies are not 'neutral' flesh and bones, but a site of power struggles where knowledge and the constant exchange of information through encounter and interaction is evident. Erving Goffman's writing on the interaction order is a constant inspiration in this respect (*see* Anderson, 1985).

One of the key issues here then is what exactly is the status of this 'age group' that we are part of? As we all realise, it is frequently how other (often more powerful) people see us that matters in terms of our status allocation and thereby access to resources, opportunities, social justice, and so on.

In this respect then, young people's membership of, and conventional association with, age-specific groupings, could be a key factor in explaining and understanding their relatively lowly status in society.

CULTURAL CHANGE AND CONTINUITY

Sociologists have also recognised that for every change in society, in our everyday social relationships, there are also continuities. Tradition plays a big part in our lives, as a nation, as cultural groupings and individual members of a family group. The fast-moving, allsinging and dancing, popular cultures that appear to dictate people's thinking and feeling so much, are essentially surface phenomena. They are essentially the 'tomato ketchup' that is poured over the meal that we are consuming. And in many essential ways, what we are consuming is a way of life that has changed very little over many decades. It is to this continuity in power relations say, that we should be looking in order to understand why young people are regarded in the way they are. 'Once a folk devil, always a moral panic!'

I am reminded here of the ideas of Basil Bernstein (writing in the 1960s/70s) who argued that schools were 'cultural repeaters', whose main culturally conservative function was to maintain the status quo. The everyday reproduction of conventional authority as a key aspect of social hierarchy was, for Bernstein, part of the formal structuring of consciousness, including values.

VALUES AND AUTHORITY

The nature of authority is a key issue for Sociologists, of course, and we should note that authority = power + legitimation. People in positions of authority, usually as a consequence of their role(s), rely on having their use of power seen as appropriate, reasonable and acceptable. There must be consensus, agreement, around this. However, I would suggest that many young people do not agree that the exercise of power in many of the everyday relationships they have is reasonable, and so on. Young people often talk about the abuse of power that they experience and as a consequence often withdraw their stamp of legitimacy from these situations.

Sociologists regularly discuss the importance of social and cultural 'structures' that have some influence in our lives. What are the rules that seek to regulate and guide us? Who makes and maintains these rules? Whose values are consistently seen as the most important? Whose voice is the loudest in the everyday 'discourses' that we are engaged in? These questions all point toward a further vital issue, how much agency do young people actually have? Not much, is the answer, which is reflected in the need for more focus on empowerment!

We should also note that all these issues are affected by the prevailing socio-cultural factors of social class, ethnicity, gender and locality. All, in their way, are crucial realities in the complex lives of young people.

SEEN, BUT NOT (OFTEN) HEARD?

In this article I have sought to point out some of the strengths and weaknesses of recent policy and legislation with regard to young people. The new Children Act will have a significant role to play in the lives of the young, their carers, and those that work with both. Despite their fine words and some appropriate responses by policy makers, I remain sceptical about both their motives for taking action and the likelihood that these most recent interventions will be successful. Young people are consistently stereotyped, their 'voices' disregarded, and still excluded from genuine democratic participation in the strategic thinking and decision-making that directly affects their lives. Things need to change.

REFERENCES:

ANDERSON, R. J., Hughes, J.A. and Sharrock, W. W. *The Sociology Game: An Introduction to Sociological Reasoning*. Longman, 1985

ASTLEY, J. *Present Imperfect: Future Tense?* Social Review Vol.l, No.1 findings, 1991. These are the regular and extremely useful research updates from the Joseph Rowntree Foundation (www.jrf.org.uk). See, for example: 'Young people's views and experiences of growing up' (Feb. 2002), 'Young people's changing routes to independence' (Nov. 2002), 'Vulnerable young men in fragile labour markets' (March 2004).

FOUCALT, M. *The History of Sexuality.* Peregrine, 1976.

GRIFFIN, C. *'Representations of Youth: the Study of Youth and Adolescence in Britain and America'.* Polity Press, 1993.

HALL, S. and Jefferson, T. (Eds.). *Resistance Through Rituals: Youth subcultures in post-war Britain.* Hutchinson, 1976.

MIZEN, P. *The Changing State of Youth.* Palgrave, 2004.

PINI, M. *Technologies of the Self.* In Roche, J. *et al. Youth in Society.* Sage/Open University, 2004.

Transforming Youth Work. DfEE and Connexions, 2001.

WILLIS, P. *Common Culture: Symbolic work at play in the everyday cultures of the young.* Open University Press, 1990.

Zero2nineteen - monthly magazine produced by Community Care (www.zero2nineteen.co.uk).

Youth service policy making in the 1950s [1]

1987

I was recently re-reading Ferdinand Zweig's 'The British Worker' - published in 1952.[2] It was particularly interesting to look at the chapter on the young worker given all the recent enthusiasm to offer real training for the school-leavers and potential workforce. Zweig's addressed himself to the differences in values and attitudes towards work in particular and life in general, and he noted between young and old:

"One general remark can be made about working-class adolescents: that nearly all of them prefer working to being at school. . .The time between 15 and 17 is a most critical age and decides the young man's whole future. The decisive point is whether he is apprenticed to a craft or supervisory grade or not. If he fails to be apprenticed, he is left, in the great majority of cases, in the labourers' or at best in the semi-skilled men's ranks for life."

If Zweig is read in conjunction with, say, Sillitoe's *Saturday Night and Sunday Morning* (1958) or the Crowther Report: 15-18 (1959), a fascinating picture of the young worker - potential and actual - begins to appear. Of course, most of this, like other writing of the time, is actually about the young working class male; certainly this is so if we are looking at connections with the Youth Service.

"Arthur walked into a huge corridor, searching an inside pocket for his clocking-in card and noticing, as on every morning since he was fifteen - except for a two-year break in the Army - the factory smell of oil-suds, machinery, and shaved steel that surrounded you with an air in which pimples grew and prospered on your face and shoulders, that would have turned you into one big pimple if you did not spend half an hour over the scullery sink every night getting rid of the biggest bastards. What a life, he thought. Hard work and good wages and a smell all day that turns your guts." [3]

". . .Our terms of reference require us to consider changing social needs. In every aspect of education and at every stage of our thinking we have been keenly aware of the way in which social conditions, attitudes and habits affect what education can achieve. . .Two main directions of change... seem especially important for their impact on teenagers and for the way in which they define some of the objectives of educational policy. The first is the emancipation, or isolation, of the individual (it can be looked at both ways) and the rejection of traditional authority; the second, the conquest of the field of communications by the mass production techniques which were first applied to the manufacture of goods." [4]

My aim in this article is to discuss the formation of Youth Service policy in the 1950s. I am concerned with looking at the processes that lead to the formulation of *this* or *that* policy and the forces that came to bear on that formulation. Whether all of these competing and complimentary forces were realised in the eventual policies for the Youth Service is another matter, of course, and I am very anxious to explore the alternative lines of development in those years. Understandably, perhaps, a good deal of this article will be concerned with the Youth Service policy paradigm of the 1950s, but I want to set that in context.

To spread out my period of interest, it is necessary to have to look at policy discussion and formulation, the actual function of the 'Youth Service', the nature of youth - in all its heterogeneity, from at least 1939. It is commonplace to acknowledge the impact of war on public and social administration, and this is certainly the case with the Youth Service. Consideration of the war and immediate post-war period adds a considerable amount to my brief analysis of Youth Service policy making in the 1950s. I am also very conscious of the Albermarle Report [5] hanging over me as I write about the 1950s.

One of the most important issues in the formation of the Youth Service after the war was the nature of relationships between the agencies of the State - the statutory sector, and the agencies of the voluntary sector. Up to 1939 the voluntary sector was the major influence in 'youth' organisation. One of the factors that affect the eventual outcome is the role of the voluntary agencies. This article addresses the 'partnership', the post-war settlement, the co-existence and consensus that it was argued would form the impetus and basis for the Youth Service. One of the issues of the 1950s is whether or not this partnership was a viable proposition. Did the partnership survive the ups and downs of policy making in the light of changed and changing circumstances, attitudes, and so on? The answer in brief is yes and no: it was a viable proposition, but it did not survive.

A good deal of this article is devoted to an analysis of Albermarle, particularly the critical posture that the Report took in its analysis of the post-war Youth Service and the needs for the future. However, it is an all too easy trap to fall into to start with Albermarle as if what preceded that report would, of historical necessity, lead to their account in 1960. These persons, as 'individuals' and/or members of organisations and institutions, who were inextricably tied-up in the formulation of Youth Service policy between 1939 and 1959 did not do what they did in anticipation of the Albermarle Report in 1960.

Some, with the benefit of hindsight, argue that Albermarle was the nemesis, but that argument overlooks one or two interesting sub-plots.

What does concern me is the way in which Youth Service policy making has been inconsistent. One factor that I have already alluded to, and must develop here, is the manner in which the development of post-war youth, as a reality and as an ideological construct, has some bearing on the formulation of policies for 'youth in general' in areas such as education, delinquency, family, personal sexual relations, and the formulation of policies for the Youth Service in particular. These relations between actuality, ideology and policy making are complex to say the least, even given the usual difficulties that exist in sorting out fact from fiction.

I started out by suggesting that a novel (in this case *Saturday Night and Sunday Morning*) might prove useful in helping to put together an understanding of post war youth - particularly in relation to work and leisure. I should add before proceeding with any analysis of 'youth' in the 1950s that problems do exist about the telling and retelling of what it was like to be young. Moreover, we know more than enough about the changes in Youth Service policy in relation to other youth-orientated policies in recent years to underline the point that what needs to be done about youth is a moveable feast at the best of times. Given radical changes in government, as was the case in 1979, matters can at times take a more decisive lurch in one direction or another.

At certain moments in the history of the Youth Service, and this is certainly true of the 1939-45 period, an ideal position is formulated by the policy makers, matters of principle are stated, only to be retreated from fairly quickly. It is interesting to assess all factors that brought the war-time state to create a set of policies and encourage a range of institutional developments and then more or less drop them. It is also important to emphasise that the 'creation' of the Youth Service in the war years set the seal on many years of work by many professionals working in this field of social service. It also, importantly, legitimated a whole new era of professional development, which in turn has been affected by the ups and downs in the Youth Service.

Between 1939 and the issue of the Board of Education circular 1486, 'In the Service of Youth', and 1960, and the publication of the Albermarle Report on the Youth Service in England and Wales, the orientation of the Youth Service appears to change. In 1939 there was an attempt to move away from earlier but relevant concerns with physical fitness to one of integrating the young (officially, 15-20 years) into society. This project attempted to give the young a more adult role to play in the community, especially in the 'post-war' reconstruction of society and social life.

Essentially related to this was the drive to integrate and coordinate the various strands of provision for the young already in existence.

It appears that the policy makers were appreciative of the effort made by the numerous voluntary bodies, but were anxious to see this consolidated and broadened via funding and centralisation by the State.

By the end of the 1950s, this project had apparently gone sour. The Youth Service was, ideologically, in disarray. Why did this happen? What forces were at work between 1939 and the late '50s that influenced, even dictated the change in State Policy? How did youth and society change in that fifteen-year, post-war period that led Albermarle to initiate the change of policy and set into motion the so-called 'bricks and mortar' phase of the Youth Service? Did this change represent a contraction in the aims of the State, of the policy makers?

It may well be that the condition of youth was such that the State did not feel it essential to provide a

41

service of any kind, but especially one that underwrote the integrative role of the agents of socialisation and social control in society. Perhaps there was a general belief that youth would represent a threat to order, or become a distinctive social problem, and that little or nothing had to be done about the special provisions demanded in a later phase by Albermarle?

Did Albermarle mark recognition of the separateness of youth, socially and culturally and bring to a close the period when a belief existed in society that youth could be successfully incorporated and integrated into the normative order of proper adult society? It is certainly possible to perceive the development of a discourse that increasingly marginalises youth, culturally and ideologically, and the association of youth with the creation and reproduction of deviant categories.

It is also necessary to stress the influence of the general post-1944 developments in 'Welfare' provision. It is necessary to do this because if I am to attempt to assess the magnitude of social and cultural change that has affected youth and Youth Service policy, the affects of the welfare provision on post-war British society is clearly a substantial factor and germane to my discussion. Not the least of my concerns here is the role of the expenditure controls in the Youth Service.

Whatever sums of money were envisaged in 1939 to set up and run the Youth Service were either not sufficient - or were quite drastically cut back during the following years. No matter how admirable and nec-essary the Service may have been in the eyes of successive governments, they were not prepared to make a financial commitment even in line with the fairly modest targets of war years. It is certainly true that Albermarle saw this shortfall of funds as a major factor in the failings of the Youth Service. While this appears to be true, a reductionist approach must be avoided here at the expense of a more culturally complex argument.

Before looking at the 1950s in much more detail, it is useful to look forward to Albermarle and back to the war.

Initially, to place Albermarle's project in a context, the report begins with the 'conventional wisdom' criteria for the Committee's work.

"We were appointed at a most crucial time. First, because several aspects of national life, to which the Youth Service is particularly relevant, are today causing widespread and acute concern. These include serious short-term problems, such as that of the 'bulge' in the adolescent population. They include also much more complex and continuous elements of social change, elements to which adolescents are responding sharply and often in ways which adults find puzzling or shocking. Secondly, because it soon became clear to us that the Youth Service itself is in a critical condition." [6]

What emerges from Albermarle is that many people within the political policy making and professional bureaucratic elites had dedicated them-selves to the development of a comprehensively more effective, national Youth Service. They were dis-appointed at the failure to achieve this ideal. Whether they were naive to believe that the relatively adventurous goals set in the 1939-1945 period could be achieved is another matter. It is not uncommon for groups of well-informed and sincerely motivated professionals to pursue goals in their chosen field with a certainty of their appropriateness and successful achievement, which is not matched by the policy makers in general. One of the features of the period between 1945 and 1960 is the way in which the aims of the Youth Service devotees were gradually eroded, so that by 1960 there is almost the sense of having to start the project over again. As Jeffs has pointed out, the setbacks were perhaps too numerous to sustain the 'project' in any unified form at all; this may have been particularly true of cuts in funding after 1945. [7]

Sir John Maud, who was Permanent Secretary to the Ministry of Education in 1951, spoke on two related aspects of the Youth Service in that year. Firstly he warned 'the Youth Service' that those concerned with it could only expect a reduction in their already dwindling resources and a reducing share of education expenditure in the future. He also spoke of the 'raw deal' that the Youth Service had had. In this, as in other contemporary assessments of the Youth Service's relative decline, there is almost a sense of betrayal.

"In 1951 the King George's Jubilee Trust called a two-day conference at Ashbridge to debate the 'Youth Service of Tomorrow'. By then it was apparent that the expansion that had seemed a real possibility in the early and mid 1940s was not going to take place. . .The report of the conference makes somewhat sombre reading: it talks of declining membership and seemingly intractable problems 'of not enough money, not enough buildings, and too few people as leaders', as policy of fewer organisations and fewer organisers and administrators." [8]

This conference, which brought together represen-tatives from voluntary organisations and local authorities, was an explicit attempt to influence prevailing Government attitudes and policy-making. The State had been instrumental in bringing the two wings of the 'Youth Service' together and, so it seemed, let them down together. This was clearly a post-1945 judgement by Government, as all the indicators in 1939 and even in 1944, were that the 'marriage' of the voluntary and the statutory sectors would actually improve the conditions and future prospects of the 'Youth Service'.

In many ways those people from the voluntary sector could feel justified in feeling lulled into a false sense of security and being 'mugged' along the way. However, the 'mugger' was clearly 'the State', or more precisely Governments 'of the day', as those within the Local Authorities who had been drawn into partnership with the voluntary agencies were equally as dedicated to the Service and as equally dismayed, upset and disappointed by the changes in attitude and policy.

This relationship of the two sectors of the Service is certainly important in terms of the period after Albermarle, where gradually the dominance and influence of the voluntary sector is reduced in favour of the role of Local Authorities. But up to 1939 and certainly between 1939 and 1960, the voluntary sector remained the 'senior' partner.

Before 1945, the voluntary service was, to all intents and purposes, the Youth Service. The gradual development of a statutory Service during the war years made little significant change and, indeed, in the years that followed the war the relationship between the two remained an ambiguous one. Despite their evident difficulties there was a sense that the Youth Service was here to stay. Authorities and voluntary bodies responded vigorously, in spite of early difficulties of adjustment, and a creditable measure of cooperation was achieved. The Service was written about and youth workers of the time spoke of the interest and enthusiasm of the public. Universities and university colleges offered training courses for professional leaders and as the war ended the Service seemed full of promise.

However, as Eggleston points out, the seeds of the takeover were evidently sown in this war-time phase of establishing the partnership and encouraging cross-fertilisation of sectors, through the application of a fairly common ideology.

"Through the fifties the development of the statutory service continued, often in association with a parallel development of further education facilities. Though, as with all other educational development, progress varied with the prevailing economic conditions. Nonetheless, the statutory service was still considered in many areas to serve a gap-filling role: certainly it was not in any sense in competition with the established voluntary organisations, though the very existence of an alternative set of provisions had an unquestionable effect on the voluntary bodies." [9]

The Albermarle report reflects this development of partnership and also underlines the feeling of optimism that prevailed in the new Youth Service constituency despite the obvious problems that were in existence.

"In 1939 the Board of Education called the Youth Service into being with the issue of a single circular. This could not have happened but for what had gone before. . .What the Board did at the start of the war was to bring. . .three parties, State, education authority and voluntary organisation, into a working arrangement to which the term 'Youth Service' has ever since been given".

In Circular 1486 the Board undertook "a direct responsibility for youth welfare". The President had set up a National Youth Committee and local education authorities were called on to set up youth committees of their own. Key phrases in the circular were: "close association of local education authorities and voluntary bodies in full partnership in a common enterprise" . . . "ordered scheme of local provision". . "indicate the lines on which a real advance can be made under more favourable conditions". . ."new constructive outlets". Later circulars made it clear that the Board regarded the Youth Service as a permanent part of education. So did the White Paper on Education Reconstruction (1943), which gave a separate section to the Youth Service. The McNair Report (1944) encouraged the public to think of youth leadership as a profession, which ought to have proper conditions of training and service. The Youth Advisory Council (the successor to the National Youth Committee) produced two reports (1943 and 1945), which were full of hope for the future of the Service. Finally the Education Act, 1944, not only made it a duty on authorities to do what they were already doing out of goodwill, but offered in addition, the county college, a mighty ally to the Youth Service.

In 1945, the Ministry of Education made it plain that they did not intend for the present to put into effect the McNair recommendations about youth leaders. All the same, the outlook still seemed bright enough to attract numbers of able men and women leaving the armed forces into the courses for professional leaders offered by universities and voluntary organisations. For two or three years longer the Service made some progress. It continued to be widely discussed and four of the Ministry's pamphlets published between 1945 and 1949 took it into serious account. Then the wind began to blow cold. With one economic crisis after another the Ministry could do no more than indicate that the Youth Service (with other forms of "learning for leisure") must be held back to allow, first, for the drive for new school places and later for the development of technical education. The county college looked as far off as ever. The Jackson Committee (1949) and the Fletcher Committee (1951) produced reports on the training and conditions of service of professional youth leaders. Neither was put into effect. The flow of recruits shrank, the number of full-time leaders fell away and the university and other full-time courses closed down one by one until today only three survive. With the Ministry unable to give the signal for advance, certain authorities lost heart. Public interest flagged, too, and not surprisingly voluntary bodies felt the effect. It is easy to over-expose the picture and to fail to do justice to the good and valiant work that has been done since the war and is still being done. All the same the Youth Service has not been given the treatment it hoped for and thought it deserved and has suffered in morale and public esteem in consequence. (10)

It is important to recognise the ideological argument bound up in this statement by Albermarle. It retains the notion of the 'post-war', especially 1944, concern with the achievement of political consensus.

The 'reality' of embourgeoisement convergence and relative affluence came later and cannot be easily reduced in cause and effect to the achievement of consensus. What is particularly significant about the 1944 Education Act is that it provided the institutionalised framework and context for the continuing discourse about schooling, and life after school, to the exclusion of other strategies. (11)

The particular relevance of this for the Youth Service was that the opportunity was created for a new liaison between State and voluntary provision and that the *need* for a service to enhance the emerging obsessions with 'character building' and 'citizenship' was legitimated by the State's legislative intervention. The 'universatising' character and intention of educational legislation gave an impetus for the job of citizenship-building to be carried on and developed beyond the limits of the school. Where the project eventually failed was that, despite the encouraging words from the Board and Ministry of Education and in the 1944 Act, the Governments of the fifties were not at all sure that the *reinforcement* role of the Youth Service was really necessary.

I would argue that it is important to consider the influence of existing institutional values, structures and practices of the long established youth clubs and organisations in influencing or determining policy making. Equally as important in its own way is to recognise the influence of the range of quasi-scientific notions of adolescence in both the 1944 Act and the emergence of the Youth Service.

Board of Education circular 1516 (ref. 27.6.40) [12] set the tone for the new Youth Service in emphasising the character-building role of the Service in tandem with the drive for citizenship *within* the free liberal association framework of the new pluralist society. It was implicit that this was training for the necessary adult role acceptance to maintain the normative order. What is more explicit in the official literature of the

1940s is the concern with the 'indirect' nature of this socialisation. Yes, of course Youth Service workers were agents of socialisation and social control, but their role was not seen to be a coercive one. Indeed, the widely held assumption was that a coercive role would not be needed as young people would naturally gravitate to the Service that provided them with the dual opportunity to sit at the feet of their elders and share with their peers the various recreational activities that would bring pleasure and a greater understanding of their part in society.

Wolfenden was the first chairman of the Youth Advisory Council appointed by the President of the Board of Education in 1942 to advise on matters relating to the Youth Service. Wolfenden is linked with two crucial documents establishing the tone of the service. These two reports, ('The Youth Service after the War' 1943 and 'The Purpose and Content of the Youth Service' 1945-HMSO), [13] discussed the need for a Service, the role of youth in the war, the nature of the 'curriculum' to be offered, even the kind of leadership required. These Reports have a tone that reflects the influence of public school and grammar school values.

Indeed, Wolfenden was the Headmaster of Uppingham School in 1943 and of Shrewsbury School by 1945. The 1943 Report placed great store on the courage of the young in the war and looking beyond the end of hostilities anticipated the continued fortitude of the younger generation.

"We are convinced that they will respond to the challenge of the post-war world just as courageously as they have met the challenge of war, if only they can be offered as careful and thorough a training for citizenship as they are now given for battle. Given such training, we believe that the great majority of them will grow up to be individuals physically, mentally and spiritually capable of playing their full part as adult members of the kind of society we wish to see, that is, a society which can only function effectively if all its members take an informed and responsible share in its activities". (14)

One interesting aspect of this 'training and citizenship' business is the development, both welcomed and alarming, of armed forces education, which we know enough about to see what a significant influence it had on the 1945 General Election and beyond. (15)

The 1943 report anticipated a post-war plurality that must have scared many sections of the British elite. Many of those in custody of the great British heritage of privilege and inequality could not have begun to contemplate this awful prospect.

"We neither expect nor wish all young people to grow up holding the same views, for if they did both they and the body politic would be the poorer. We want each one of them to come to see that the fullest life, both for himself and for his community, demands that he should recognise duties and responsibilities as well as enjoy rights and benefits. We want to see them all grounded in the principal loyalties of a sound civilisation; their loyalty to God, the King and Country, to their family, to their neighbour and to their unit of livelihood. We believe that bringing up young people to practise these loyalties will give disciplined freedom to society and yield what is due to both the individual and the community". [16]

This path of development for the formation of young persons' values, attitudes and behaviour is complemented by the functions of the Youth Service itself. Of some interest here is the clearly expressed view that some young persons would be developed and guided by their schooling and career aims, their inheritance or cultural capital. The perceived model of upper and middle class education as an agency of socialisation and social control is that it reproduced the inclusive nature of things. However, the situation is different for the non-academic, and by definition, working class young person, who is still faced with schooling as an agency of social control. This report warns against the problems induced by an 'over academic' development of the schooling and youth services.

"The majority of young people do not find satisfaction in an academic atmosphere even during school years... to confront them again in the Youth Service with the same academic and intellectual standards in which they could find no significance at school will drive them out of any form of youth organisation forever". [17]

The Youth Service had its foundations built on 'shifting sand', and had fallen back on its traditional mixture of *ad hoc*ism and philanthropy. The organisers and associates of the Service after 1945 did look to the Ministry of Education for a lead and for an ally in the competition and bidding for resources. This was to be a major error of judgement. Albermarle pointed to good work done, local enthusiasm and high hopes, despite the lack of support from the State.

How then, other than for purely financial reasons, can we explain the change of heart by post-war government? What I would argue is that Albermarle and the reports and discourse after 1960 indicate that a major error of judgement was made by the State.

It might well be that the State policy makers relied on an inadequate, indeed out of date, analysis of the nature of youth and society. I would want to suggest the following as part of what the government's assessment of youth seemed to omit or overlook or chose to ignore and put the discussion on policy making made above into a wider context.

A large body of sociological writing since the 1950s has emphasised one of the most significant changes in the life of the industrial population: that of the movement from work to leisure. This movement has not only been in terms of hours per week devoted to work or non-work activities, but to a re-orientation in the advanced industrial societies towards the prime pursuit of leisure, enjoyment and recreation. The 'leisure consumers' have become vitally important to the creation of wealth in industrial society. Again this development is part of wider, even more far reaching changes. Firstly, it is evident in the movement away from industrial societies dominated by manufacturing production to ones greatly influenced, if not yet dominated, by service industry; and, secondly, in the major movement away from concentration on the problems of production to those of consumption. This series of fundamental changes are usually referred to as post-industrialism and post-scarcity. The latter concept celebrates the point of development in industrial society when the advances in technology related to altered production organisation has provided the opportunity for vast numbers of people to be released from time in the workplace. Larkin[18] makes great play with the fact of a significant shift from cultural emphasis on 'work time' to cultural emphasis on leisure, but, even he fails to underline the fact that the societal development of leisure was also, essentially, an economic development. The expansion in the leisure 'industries', most, but not all, in the service sector, has been one of the most significant areas of corporately managed economic expansion since the 1950s. Indeed, I would argue that this development is a further episode in social reproduction in the advanced industrial societies. Clearly the very living-out of leisure, the consumption that takes place in this time and, largely, the values associated with its prosecution are ways in which the forces and relations of production in society are reproduced and maintained. [19]

There is an 'illusion' of freedom in the cultural ambiance of leisure that is a marked aspect of its ideological character. However, as Larkin also suggests, post-war youth essentially part of the process whereby desires have replaced needs. This cultural change is part of, not separate from, the development of post-industrial, post-scarcity society where 'youth' as a social formation has been created. Youth, as a *socially* constructed formation arrived simultaneously, indeed largely as a consequence of, these other social and economic changes.

The official reports dealing with the emergence and development of a Youth Service in the UK reflect the contradictions and confusions that arise from these changes. The various reports, up to and including Albermarle, concentrate on the functional necessity of adequate socialisation on the one hand, while also recognising the disequilibria caused by 'adolescence' on the other. However, the concern with personal physiological and psychological development neglects the changed 'world' in which young people are 'growing up'.

It is not my intention to enter into a lengthy account of the emergence of post-war 'youth', but what is certainly significant is that the policy makers either did not understand the nature of the arrival of 'youth', or indeed *did* have an inkling of what was happening and chose not to communicate their thoughts publicly. Certainly by the time of Albermarle, the policy makers in the field of the Youth Service did realise that most of the post-war project had gone dreadfully wrong, the Youth Service was, according to Albermarle, moribund, unresponsive and dying on its feet.

Albermarle tried to set the Youth Service on a new course, away from an agency of socialisation that focused attention upon the inculcation of traditional bourgeois values (loyalty to God, King and Country, family, neighbour, employer and private property), to a Service that not only recognised the plurality of the post-war social structure, and the uniqueness of 'youth', but also sought to both retreat behind youth club doors, entertaining the young into conformity while offering what specialist assistance and advice the young were prepared to seek or take.

Fyvel is typical of many critics of post-war youth writing at the time of Albermarle. [20] One of the central features of Fyvel's analysis was the shock he registered on behalf of many adults that an increasing number of young people were deviant despite all that was on offer in the post-1950 welfare state world. Fyvel wrote a reassessment of his book in 1978, which offers an interesting insight into his more explicit thesis.

What I saw as finally crumbling by the fifties was the classical bourgeois capitalist society dominated by the urban middle class. This society consolidated its status in the 19th century and was based on exclusive upper middle class economic privilege, buttressed by domestic servants. It was filled with institutions and patriarchal figures embodying moral authority.

By the 'fifties, this society was being rapidly replaced by the British consumer society".

"So, but more slowly, was its system of moral authority; deference to upper class and state authority; to employers, the law, the police, the churches and teachers and to parents in the family which had held society together. A new authority was assumed by the advertisers, entertainers and other hedonistic voices of the consumer society". [21]

I would therefore re-emphasise the disjuncture that exists between the social and cultural forces that comprise the framework of the Youth Service. The role of Government has been interventionist but changeable. The partnership of statutory local authority and voluntary agencies has always been an uncertain, localised and ambiguous affair. Some LEAs have done much to cement the post-war foundations; others, as Albermarle pointed out, took fright or became greedy for influence and set off in their own direction. Collectively, these agencies have tended to dictate the aims and objectives of the Youth Service and assumed or hoped that it would attract the usage of the young. As I have argued above, the various agencies overlooked too much to be remotely successful and when faced with the recalcitrance of pusillanimousness of youth, fell back on traditional irrational authoritarianism to resolve their problems. The socialisation process of society assumes enormous contradictions in those conditions. (22)

It is now appropriate to expand my assessment of the 1950s developments in the Youth Service, set against the paradigm of Youth in that period and what actually seems was happening then.

I have already cited the Crowther Report and it is worth devoting more time to it. There is an element of the mass culture debate running through this Report. The liberality of the new age is clearly a cause for rejoicing and concern. It is all very well to open up new frontiers for the young, but the consequent changes may not always be those desired by the Establishment. "Emancipation and the moral code" therefore features as a destructive issue and concern in Crowther. There are, for example, changes in the nature of the family. What Fletcher [23] and other sociologists of the 1950s were to call the democratisation of the family is seen by Crowther as a mixed blessing. Older teenagers "are no longer beholden to their parents for their pleasures". [24] Levels of expectations amongst the young have changed, as have staying-in and going-out patterns. The Report points to a break up of the traditional moral order, which in turn, of course, affects the family and its significance as an agent of socialisation and social control. Needless to say, the thorny issue of sexual ethics is raised and significantly enough is run into a substantial consideration of juvenile delinquency. Mays [25] and even worse, Burt, [26] are taken as markers for an analysis of the factors leading to a steady increase in delinquency. Mays is quoted, for example, as underlining one central problem of the 1950s for the Establishment, that the young are not only deviant, they are also defiant! A good many issues are rolled up together here, for example, the pressure on the traditional community, the effects of the war on children, the lack of relevance in schooling for older children. The Crowther Report argues that in the past a man stuck loyally to the tradition, custom and practice of his father and only changed in dire circumstances, but in the 1950s, people are giving up their old loyalties. This is certainly true of the young and once again the unfortunate influences of the media are cited.

It is interesting here to reflect upon the mass culture debate in conjunction with delinquency and the like. Fyvel always argued that the liberal establishment were shocked by the disagreeable and ungrateful nature of the young in the 1950s. Despite all the wonders of the welfare state, the young, or significant sections of it anyway, remained disaffected and recalcitrant. The glitter of the emergent pop culture, in its wider sense, upset the establishment (in schools and elsewhere) and they were right to suspect that they were fighting a losing battle. They were, of course, not prepared to fight the entrepreneurs of the new world media head on; instead, they preferred to attempt to dilute the product, or distract the potential audience/activists. They failed.

The American experience of this problem came earlier and was different in the sense that the salesmanship, consumption, acquisitiveness and status -obsessed culture was instrumental in the formation of the media. Randall Jarrell was able to write in the early 1960s with absolute certainty that,". . .inside every fat man there is a man who is starving, part of you is being starved to death and the rest of you is being stuffed to death". [27] Crowther put it much more in terms of the passage of a golden era of adult authority:

". . .all that has happened is the substitution of the public opinion of their peers for the wisdom of the ages. Teenage opinion is often badly informed, fickle and superficial. How should it be otherwise? Of all age-groups, the teenagers are most exposed to the impact of the 'mass media' of communication".[28]

Crowther asserts that the confluence of new demands, pressures, situations and tastes, places an extra burden of responsibility on the local authority to provide support for the young.

"The teenagers with whom we are concerned need, perhaps before all else, to find a faith to live by. They will not all find precisely the same faith and some will not find any. Education can and should play some part in their search. It can assure them that there is something to search for and it can show them where to look and what other men have found". [29]

Crowther rests its case in this segment of its influence by arguing that society ought not to withdraw from the young worker the help it gave to the school student.

The late 1950s and early 1960s was an interesting period of reforming legislation particularly in relation to what Stuart Hall and others have called, the legislation of consent.[30] The Home Secretary-ships of Butler and Jenkins were marked by an attempt to direct growing public concerns about personal and inter-personal liberality into parliamentary action. The theme of moral panics is clearly to be identified in this period, with periods of panic reasonably well related to significant issues and events of the hour. Certainly the mobilisation of bias is a significant issue in these years and besides anything else that might be considered it is fruitful to look at what was being argued for and against youth and the Youth Service within the politics of reform. The importance of residual and emergent values cannot be over-estimated here, in piecing together a picture of the case being put for and against the development of the Youth Service.

It would seem, for example, that the increasingly interventionist 'state' of the 1950s deliberately chose to bifurcate youth issues, by setting the normal sharply apart from the abnormal. There was the tendency then to deal with youth in a way that reinforced the idea that the troublemakers, the disaffected and so on, could and should, be regarded as a special category of young persons. Delinquency, for example, increasingly becomes a 'way of life' for a minority from the State's perspective of young persons and not a 'fact of life' for the majority. The interventionist State's 'policy', administrative strategy of isolation, ghettoisation of social problems as a practical means of dealing with youth issues is increasingly marked.

In conclusion, let me attempt to draw together some of the threads of my arguments on the emergence of a State sanctioned, if not always State financed and run Youth Service. Throughout this article I have stressed the war-time and immediate post-war context of public and social administration in relation to the development of ideas about what form work on creating a Youth Service could and should take. Hopefully I have emphasised the mixture of hopeful openness and continued desire for social control processes in the collective minds of the administrators, *etc.*, of the time. The reconstruction of Britain, in so many senses that do not need elaborating here, certainly includes major discussion throughout society about the nature of economic and social relations and the desired nature of social change to bring about the 'new and good society'.

The social democratic/pluralist faith in the evolutionary democratisation of society is a central focus of debate here, particularly with regard to the working class. What part were 'they' to play, be allowed to play, *etc.*, in the shaping of post-war society? Changes to and within the working class are, by definition, part of the material for discussion. It may well have been the case that those persons and classes with power to shape the future of society assumed that the working class share of power or life chances or whatever, would remain much the same; they would just have a more comfortable life perhaps? Less of their children would go hungry and die young? More of their young would go a little beyond the four Rs? More young adults would obtain and retain a job, pay their national insurance, have a not too overcrowded and damp-free place to live? As we all know, the place where the vision of the 'Brave New World' for all and the Consumer(ised) Society meet, was, have become, an unholy mess.

The post-war generation of young persons and those engaged in the development of young persons and those engaged in the development of the Youth Services were, whether they were self-conscious of it or not, right in the thick of this. The cultural/political struggles that took place; or even, of course, crucially perhaps, *did* not take place, at the end of the War, left their indelible mark on the Youth Service that emerged.

The debate about the fate of the Working Class and the Working Class Community in the light of all these desired and imposed, struggled for and reluctantly conceded, changes, has been a considerable one.[31] The analysis of Youth Service policy making should be seen as contributing to, and learning from, this broader debate.

REFERENCES AND NOTES:

1. This article first appeared in *Youth and Policy* No. 19, 1987.
2. ZWEIG, F. *The British Worker.* Penguin, 1952.
3. SILLITOE, A. *Saturday Night and Sunday Morning.* Pan, 1958.
4. CROWTHER REPORT. (15 to 18) Min. of Ed. HMSO, 1959 *p.36.*
5. ALBERMARLE. Min. of Ed. *The Youth Service in England and Wales.* HMSO, 1960.
6. *Ibid.*
7. JEFFS, A. J. *Young People and The Youth Service.* RKP, 1979.
8. *Ibid p.29.*
9. EGGLESTON, J. *Adolescence and Community. The Youth Service in Britain.* Arnold, 1976, *p.16.*
10. Albermarle *op. cit.*
11. BARON, S. et. al. *Unpopular Education. Schooling and Social Democracy in England, 1944-1981.* Hutchinson, 1981.
12. Board of Education Circular 1516. HMSO, 1940.
13. Board of Education. *The Youth Service after the War.* (The first). Report of the Youth Advisory Council. HMSO, 1943. Ministry of Education. *The purpose and Content of the Youth Service.* (The second) Report of the Y.A.C. HMSO, 1945. J. WOLFENDON was chairman for both Reports.
14. *Ibid p.5/6.*

15. GRANT, N. *Citizen Soldiers: Army Education in World War 2. in Formations of Nation and People.* Ed. by Bennett, T. *et al* RKP, 1984.

16. Board of Education. 1943. *Op cit* p.6.

17. *Ibid p.10.*

18. LARKIN, R.W. *Suburban Youth in Cultural Crisis.* OUP, 1979.

19. CLARK, J. and CRITCHER, C. *The Devil Makes Work. Leisure in Capitalist Britain.* MacMillan, 1985.

20. FYVEL, T.R. *The Insecure Offenders: Rebellious Youth in the Welfare State.* Penguin, 1961.

21. FYVEL, T.R. *The 'Insecure Offenders' in retrospect.* New Society, (20.7.78, p.128.)

22. See ASTLEY, J. *Industrial-Urban Culture, Youth and the Problem of Socialisation.* in The Social Science Teacher, Vol.8, No.2, 1978.

23. FLETCHER, R. *Family and Marriage in Britain.* Penguin, 1962.

24. Crowther Report. *op cit* p.36.

25. MAYS, J. *The Young Pretenders.* Sphere, 1969.

26. BURT, C. *The Young Delinquent.* ULP, 1969.

27. JARRELL, R. *A Sad Heart at the Supermarket.* Farrar, Straus & Giroux, 1962.

28. Crowther Report. *op cit* p.43.

29. *Ibid* p.44.

30. HALL, S. *Reformism and the Legislation of Consent in Permissive-ness and Control: the fate of the Sixties Legislation. Edited by* J. Clark *et al.* MacMillan, 1980.

31. See for example: Clark, J. *et al. Working Class Culture. Studies in history and theory.* Hutchinson, 1979. George, V. and Wilding, P. *Ideology and Social Welfare.* RKP, 1976. Hoggart, R. *The Uses of Literacy.* Penguin, 1958. Rojeck, C. *Capitalism and Leisure Theory.* Tavistock, 1985. Seabrook, J. *What went wrong?* Gollancz, 1978. *A World Still to Win. The Reconstruction of the Post-War Working Class* (with Trevor Blackwell), faber & faber, 1985.

65

Being an agent of change: young people, democracy and cultural change

1992

"Youth issues move up the political agenda" argued David Brindle in his Guardian article on 4.12.91. His view was based largely on the Prime Minister's preparedness to listen to the case being put by the British Youth Council for a greater role in decision making by young people. A good deal of enthusiasm is attached to the idea of a ministry of youth - with cross-departmental responsibilities - much in the same way as advocated for women's concerns in the past.

The BYC has developed a 'Youth Rights Manifesto', which covers a considerable range of 'political/citizens rights', issues from Education and Training to safe-guarding the environment. However, this well-meaning approach does still see 'political' in a narrow, establishment politics way. Where, for example, is there any reference to young people's rights over their choice of culture activity, valued knowledge(s) and ideas and their access to resources and amenities to be creative?

For me, these issues about rights, decision making and access, questions about authority and choices are part of long running arguments about elite cultures and the desire of small, exclusive social groups to impose their values on us all. This is especially the case for young people's lives and is an aspect of social control as far as I am concerned.

In two recent, and linked, publications, Paul Willis extends this argument on the dominance of elite cultures and the irrelevance of these 'educational' and artistic values for most people's lives. Willis is arguing for a greater acknowledgement (and funding) of what he calls 'Common Culture' (Willis, 1990).

Put simply, Willis is saying that young people do have a vibrant, creative and valuable diversity of culture. They are engaged in a wide range of social processes creating and using for their own purposes, cultural and artistic products. Of course this is related to identity shaping and expression and is certainly political in the sense that any self-conscious action to create a distinctive and semi-autonomous culture is political. Where this all becomes political is in the debates about the apportioning of value to cultures and the allocation of resources.

Willis is also extending a view that he developed about schooling in *Learning to Labour* (1978). There, he suggested that the rejection of the elitist school culture by working class 'lads' was a mini critique of the capitalist ethos. This ethos suggests that the main and valued route to high status occupation was via a 'good education'. Willis' 'lads' reject this for the confidence trick (dominant ideology) that it is. The 'lads' pursued their own anti-scholastic culture in their own way rendering the ideological messages redundant.

In *Common Cultures*, Willis is once again suggesting that the overwhelming rejection (or lack of engagement with) elite, Bourgeois Culture by most young people is a critique of Bourgeois aesthetics and values. Again this is political and is reminiscent of the argument that popular cultures in society are the site of struggles between contending groups. Because it is the terrain of popular cultures, including the mass media, that most people travel over in their daily lives, there are real attempts by different groups to conquer the cultural 'high ground' and profess their authority. Much of this professing is to do with which cultures should or should not be resourced, developed, opened, closed, *etc*. This is particularly significant when it comes to the allocation of public funds via the various agencies of the British State.

My own concept of Ideological Culture Apparatuses (ICA) is also useful here. I have attempted to identify why and how the State and other agencies, like commercial ones, have allocated values and resources to certain cultural activities. The current Arts Council strategy debate is an interesting example of the politics of funding. The current 'debate' is supposedly engaging us citizens in decision making about the allocation of public funds. However, this activity is as minority and marginal as the use of these debated-over 'artistic' cultural products are themselves. For the lives of most (young) people the current debate about who should get 'the crumbs falling from the Bourgeois culture table' is as irrelevant and exclusive as the activities themselves.

If we are going to engage in a debate about what value is placed on cultural action and production, we need to first and foremost acknowledge that the politics of this are based on conflict and not consensus criteria. In the main, cultural pursuits of young people, 'home grown' or consumed in the 'market place', are essentially of the commercial nexus. What State funding there is continues to be a form of social, cultural and aesthetic control.

Returning to my concept of ICA, I would, of course, acknowledge that the commercial sector produces and manipulates ideas alongside the State apparatuses (*e.g.*, education). I would certainly want to debate the positive and negative aspects (as I see it) of the ideological processes that young people are engaged in daily. The role of the media in all its guises is clearly an important area for discussion amongst and with the young, but not in a top-down patronising way that epitomises the 'built-in' elitism of those with power.

These necessary discussions will take place within, or in conjunction with, various agencies. For example, plenty needs to be said about the curricula currently on offer in schools and colleges across the country. It is not only HRH the Prince of Wales who would select the Shakespeare ahead of other cultural products at the heart of the curriculum. The lives and works of the 'great and good' are championed in a very cross-curricula way to the exclusion, or down-grading, of much else. The Youth Service could do much more about the advocating of alternative perspectives on whose culture is important. The Youth Service may be better than most in giving space 'internally' to cultural diversity, but it could surely play a more vanguard role.

Access to the mass media, the most potent form of communicating in society, still remains difficult and arbitrary. More needs to be done to open up access to media resources and, crucially, to 'allow' young people to be innovative, to make mistakes and learn from them, not sticking to the conventional and safe ways. There is a degree of 'youth-ghetto' media already, but we need to go well beyond this in the democratic development of resources and amenities. If we are serious about continuing to seek a lively, dynamic and healthy democracy, it is essential to develop the participatory dimension of day-to-day politics and particularly policy making.

Two recent developments in Oxfordshire seem to me examples of good practice in the battle for 'grounded aesthetics'.

Firstly is a proposal, still in its early stages, for a community radio. It is still to be decided whether this should be located in Oxford's College of Further Education or in a local Community or Youth Centre. The broad aim is to provide an open access medium for local (in the Country areas) people to express their views in creative and innovative ways. The primary focus will be on youth, a consistently unrepresented group locally.

The second project is already well underway. This is 'Arts work', a multi-media youth issues focused project funded by public, voluntary and private sector sponsors. Specific youth service activities have already been completed, *e.g.*, making posters as part of an environmental issues campaign. The main focus, however, is on a magazine 'MAP', the first issue of which is due out in June 1992. This is what the project coordination has to say about the magazine:

"MAP has been set up to enable young people between the ages of 14-19 to find and raise their voices. It aims to chart the terrain of young people's ideas and experiences and bring them to the attention of both young and also the wider community. In order that the magazine represents young people and their opinions, they will be involved in every aspect of its production. This will include being responsible for designing pages and images and researching and writing news and feature articles. As is in keeping with such a publication, young people that participate will ultimately take control of the magazine's editorial policy and direction."

I will be keeping a close eye on these developments, both out of general youth work interest and also because of my specific concerns about agency and change discussed in this article. I look forward to reporting on their success in the near future.

REFERENCES:
WILLIS, P., Learning to Labour, Saxon House, 1978
WILLIS, P., *Common Cultures*, Open University Press, 1990.
WILLIS, P., *Moving Cultures*, Calouste Gulbenkian Foundation, 1990

'Catch the Blue Train. . . '- knowing about youth and music

1988

> *"I'm a man with a clear destination*
> *I'm a man with a broad imagination*
> *You fog my mind, you stir the soul*
> *I can't find... no control...*
> *Catch the blue train..."*[1]

Whenever I walk into a record shop, I still experience a sense of excitement, of anticipation. The constant flow of music acts as a back-drop to the communications that are taking place therein. Sometimes something special is on the turntable and this invariably adds to the tension that makes this act of conspicuous consumption that much more significant.

For example, the other day I walked into one of my regular shops to be met by Robbie Robertson 'down some crazy river' in search of body and soul - it was, as usual, enough to send a shiver down my spine.

Buying records continues to be a pleasurable, recreational act for me within a network of social and cultural-communicative relations that at one and the same time is an individual act, a choice, but also part of a general and even, given the cultural nature of things, a collective act. I consistently ride my two horses; the self-conscious sociologist of cultural relations and artefacts; the critic of popular and pop music/culture.

But I am also a fan; a self-conscious, discriminating fan of course, but also a defender of the faith!

The faith I keep is with the simple notion, conviction, that pop music can and does convey to me (and others) significant meanings about life and liberty. It is an orchestration of my feelings, mental and physical, underlying, overlaying my sense of place, conveying identity of sorts. Despite whatever my idiosyncratic values and tastes may be, I know for a fact that this testimony to my faith is certainly not a unique formulation, but most certainly a certain 'structure of feeling'. Indeed, it seems evident to me that many of my generation (born during or soon after the war) share an often unspoken, unwritten, but not unsung, cultural ontology. As a sociologist, I know that in order to understand who I am and where I am, *etc.*, it is necessary to come to terms with the nature of social structure and personal biography. But it is more than this: I must also realise my place in society and my role as carrier and creator of culture.

One aspect of this that I would like to develop here is to do with time and space. When we listen to pop music/songs/performers, we are also using them in an historical context, both social structurally and bio-graphically. Because of the way in which pop music is part of the processes whereby we become who we are, and how we might come to be, believe in who we are, *etc.*, we continue to use it as reference points, biographical footnotes *to our life* and social change. I hear a song from the past, I locate it and myself, I can use it as a ready device to chart the passage of personal and societal time. The music has significant resonances for me, it helps me to account for myself and for others, for time and for space. What I also do is to place value upon certain music, confer recognition of authenticity, and so on.

These separations of powers, self, culture and society - are a crucial element in understanding the formation of youth, in the past and now. What I want to discuss in this essay is the knowledge I have of being part of a certain kind of society; essentially a commercial and consumer one; and a part of certain forms of communication - of which pop music is an essential aspect - the confluence of which allows, suggests, forms a certain discourse. This is itself part of the generation relations, intra and inter, that I want to discuss along the way.

The main purpose of this essay is to discuss the relationships between pop music and the formation of youth culture(s). The convention of our time is that the relationship is self-evident and has been so since the 1950s at least. However, merely to restate what might be true is not good enough. I may, for example, suggest that capital-labour relations still dominate everyday life in the UK and that alienation has something to do with it all - but I should attempt to say *how* it happens.

The relationship between youth and music seems in sharp enough focus from a distance. When up-close things understandably perhaps, look differently. Not just in the sense of where the foci might be, but also that what becomes sharp and diffuse or blurred can change alarmingly. Illusion and reality.

The artefact of pop culture is, by definition, on the surface of life - however, what has generated it/ formed it, caused it to come about, is far from skin deep. The lives that pop *seems* to mirror, mimic, express or represent are in fact what really matters. But what must be considered as well is the way in which pop articulates what is life, what is the social, what is, can be, might become, the self. It is this that is really interesting, formidable and significant for the sociologist. This is to say that the products of the pop process are important and vital in themselves. But there is no necessity about recognising these phenomena as such. Indeed, sociologists in their enthusiasm to locate explanation in the social processes of cultural production have *explained away* much of the value of pop. Pop can (and does) take us through an amazing spectrum of the sublime to the ridiculous. Non-pop; elite-cultural products, are very weighty matters in contrast, laden down with content significance, but it is, in the main, an 'inherited' culture, it is part of the property, the cultural capital, that is passed on from one generation elite to the next. With few exceptions it remains a received culture, it is, unlike pop, not much concerned with the process, 'the journey', more concerned with the end product and its value-laden place in the constellation of acceptable mores of everyday life.

To what extent has the development of popular music since the war really been a product of young person's activity and/or commercial exploitation? To what extent have young persons been diverted from their commitment to conformity, or become conformists, as a result of their engagement with these musical phenomena? To what extent have policy makers, practitioners of institutional and administrative values seen the development of youth and music cultures as threat, diversion, *etc*? Is it that musical activity and associations are the most accessible form of self-expression for the young? Is music, in its social form, the most commonplace way that young persons can create some space for themselves in their complex network of relations? Is it that the very existence of these cultural forms (with their history) has an enabling, empowering quality and value, which *is* recognised, embraced, celebrated, feared, *etc*?

What young people are likely to experience may not be as arbitrary as what they seem to do. The sense in which the impulse of the moment, the spontaneous expression, may become the by-word of a social category, a style, is important in understanding youth. So much of the everyday lives of the young now, and in the 1950s/60s, is set within a framework of typicality and likelihood: family, neighbourhood, peers, school, youth clubs, law and order, media, workplace, romance, *etc*. These and other aspects of a young person's life both liberate and circumscribe, domesticate. Youth are not simply or merely the carriers of *existing* culture. Nor are they just the inheritors of custom and practice. It would also be wrong to suggest that they face existing, perhaps dominating, cultures and have to absorb that culture, those social roles, as part of their socialising. The accumulation of knowledge of ways of life, social practices, is more complex than that. We are all, young and old, seekers of social knowledge *and* knowledge. 'Pop', like the individual, offers theories of the world in abundance. How satisfactory they are, or how well we or 'pop' may articulate them, is another matter. How do the young get to know about the adult roles they will adopt, reject and modify? These roles must exist independently of youth actually experiencing them *as a person*. What we have here is what might be described as a vocabulary of motives. Young people have motives imputed to them; they impute motives to others and themselves. Pop music is a symbol system used by all and sundry, not just as pleasure, leisure, politics, religion, *etc.*, *etc.*, but also used as a 'battleground' of the imputing of motives for actions. How are ideas about roles, choices, life, *etc.*, to be communicated? What is quite evident is that for good or for ill, pop music is 'used' by all manner of people to convey ideas about what life is like, was like, and should be like. The construction of possibilities via pop music is as important an issue as arguing that people express themselves, collectively and individually, via pop.

I have already suggested that it is not good enough to keep restating the socio-cultural truism that the development of youth and music are interrelated. One important example of the problems here is the complementary undercurrents of cultural diversity, consensus and/or conflict over time. It is true to say that we can trace the development of the interrelation of youth and music cultures over the last four decades. But can we argue that it is possible to compare, and thereby evaluate, what is happening now with what was happening then. I think not. The picture becomes even more cluttered if we consider the role of social policy in the years since the war. No doubt the policy makers did start out with some fixed, conservative notions about the place and role of young persons in society after the war. Surprisingly enough, though, the policy makers concerned primarily with 'youth policy' were very aware of the *changed circumstances* that had come to exist in the post-war 'space'. Take, for example, the problem of sociology's response to the post-war trans-Atlantic world. I have always felt that the tension created by the structural-functionalist 'grand theorising' on the one hand and the pragmatic humanism of interpretive sociologies on the other hand has been one of the most fascinating aspects of the development of society in the 1950s. One of the key aspects of this pragmatic humanist critique of society was a concern with alienation. This alienation was seen as part and parcel of the stresses and strains of post-war western life. The rifts between social and human needs and the dominating relations of the day seemed so great that the very future of *society* was in question. Of course the pragmatic humanist movement and moment was mainly in America. However, whichever side of the Atlantic, what has interested me in respect of the youth culture is the question, How did the alienation phenomenon come to be represented in post-war pop? Is it possible to argue that the construction/production of (a mainly youth) pop music set up an alternative set of explanations and understandings 'alongside' the traditional bourgeois versions of social reality? At the heart of the pragmatic humanist critique of post-war society, there is a series of questions that focus upon 'abundance for what', the nature of the 'organisation man', and the 'lonely crowd'. These are questions (which conjure up) the spectre of the alienated human at odds with modern or advanced society. A view of modern 'man', old and young, symbolically dislocated, seemingly torn out of the context of the social institutions on which 'he' depends. Self and institutional order no longer mesh. This has innumerable resonances in the politics of pleasure, the doped mass, the mass culture and the commodification of creativity.

The out-pouring of pop from the 1950s seems to be the very antithesis of this humanist critique most of the time. If the 'devil' was capitalism, bureaucratic elitism, consumerism, the commercial nexus, then pop music and those associated in all manner of producing and consuming ways, seemed clearly in league with the horned one! But was this ever entirely true? Does this 'bracket away' any alternative value?

It is voguish now to speak of youth in the 1980s as the 'lost generation'. Can we therefore assume that in using this idea, some comparison is being made with the past, with a 'found generation' perhaps? The

79

precarious liberty and liberality of the 1960s was experienced and shared in the most part by the immediate post-war born generation. The intra- and post-war reconstruction of society was not just a bricks and mortar job; it was, besides everything else, a reconstruction of culture and values. It is, as I have already indicated, significant that most of the policy making is stronger and indeed was rooted first and foremost in the dominant and dominating institutional values of the 1940s and 1950s. From the young person's point of view, the decade and a half after the war was a peculiar mish-mash of excursions and alarms. There appears, perhaps more with hindsight, to have been a path of social and cultural development to follow, but in fact, life was more 'mazelike' than anything else.

There are inevitably many ifs and buts here. If post-war British society had not moved towards a 'welfare state' on the one hand and an increasing consumer led economic expansion on the other, would young people have had what scope they did? If numerous forms of American popular culture had not penetrated UK air space so soon, would there have been the increasingly precocious musical developments here? If the collective warfare to welfare spirit had not prevailed, would there have been so much for the young to have and be resented for? (I would add here that I have many doubts about whether the UK is a 'welfare' state, rather than a 'social security' state.)

There can be little doubt that the economic and socio-political developments that took place after 1942, say, created a degree of 'space' that allowed the formation of a post-war generation of 'youth' plus the associated enthusiasm, creation, mediation, adoption, *etc.*, of distinctive looking and sounding cultures. So it could be argued that the post war generation were 'found' in possession of much lethal equipment with which to perpetrate their grotesque and dastardly deeds up to and including the 1960s. The post-war generation's *direct* effect on youth and music cultures came to an end in the mid-ish 1960s. From that point, the starting place for much of the interrelation between youth and music shifted to another site. This is not to say that the tradition, some important values, cultural patterns, *etc.*, of the post-war scene were completely thrown out; far from it. They were in a residual culture sense relocated within the aspects of emergent pop, youth and music cultures that developed.

One of the issues of the post-war period is that the emergence of youth and pop music cultures seemed to undermine the classless nature of British society. We know, of course, that this is not strictly true. We have experienced the American phenomenon for treating stratification as an issue of occupationally led status ranking. This view, there and here, placed great emphasis on liberality, diffusion, affluence, consensus and embourgeoisement. This is not to say that class did not figure in the assessments of social and cultural development on both sides of the Atlantic, it did, but the focus had turned away from conflict, an 'end of ideology'.

In the UK, the most interesting writing on class formation, consciousness and cultures was being written 'outside' of sociology to a great extent. [2] A good deal of emphasis was being placed on the changing circumstances of the working class, focusing particularly interestingly from my point of view on the crisis of working class hegemony, or on the cultural imperialism of the middle and entrepreneurial classes. There is an undercurrent in much of this writing (particularly in the 1950s and early 1960s) which suggests that the working class - and even more so (?), their political leaders - colluded in their own cultural subordination.[3] There is a sense here that the educational values of the 1950s and early 1960s, for example, inadequately prepared the working class for the problems which lay ahead. There are echoes here of the timeless radical demand for an education to create/provide 'really useful knowledge'. But the lesser of these issues was the question of non-work time and the ways in which the young (working class males in the main) might develop leisure activities in a part response to their newly found status in society.

What is particularly important here is the detail of the relationship between the young and leisure. [4] It seems immaterial what point of the 1950s-80s is considered because what can be seen is an extremely complicated network of interrelations between young persons, their families, neighbourhoods, schools, workplaces, leisure-time places, the media in general, but music(s) and the social/cultural practices of the music industry, in particular. Of course what the 'surface' looks like at any one time is greatly affected by fads and fashions, but it is also affected by the processes that formed and reforms post-war popular and pop culture. I do not have any doubts about the relative autonomy of much of popular and pop culture over the last thirty years or so. [5] Indeed one of the more interesting aspects of this phenomenon is the relation between fact and fiction in any writing about these years.

An important (and currently very notable) aspect of much of the best fiction writing over the post-war years - prose, essays, poetry, films, *etc.* - is to use, intersperse in the text, "extracts from real life". [6] This takes many forms of history; texts, documentary, visual images, sounds, and so on. However, it should be remembered that this 'real' history (in whatever form) is, in fact, constructed or manufactured; selected, edited, deliberately formed through juxtaposition, compassion and so on. In short, it has an ideology. . . an ideology of 'authenticity'. It has also been formed under certain sets of circumstances for certain purposes, using as often as not, conventionalised, often 'transparent' means of doing so. This juxtaposition of fact and fiction is not only significant in terms of its appearance together, but also in the assumptions of 'writer and reader' about the nature of the *parts and the whole*. Take any example of the rise to fame and fortune of a pop band/musician of the 50s and 60s onwards. 'Beatlemania' is, by definition, a testimony to the significance of story telling in the formation of reality. If we look at films like *That'll be the Day*, it is inevitable that fact or fiction will overlap and so on; even more so *A Hard Day's Night*! (7)

In the kaleidoscopic formation of any popular or pop culture to do with youth, the tellings and retelling matters a great deal. It not only exists amongst the users, focus and so on, it gets replanted within the very music culture itself. This is most clear in the construction and replication of pop music genre like 'Romantic Love'. In all the businesses of action and reaction, signs and symbols, it is not just what people say, do, write or sing that matters, it is also whether people believe it. This in turn raises important questions about the real life processes of adoption and adaptation (that we usually refer to as socialisation) and requires us to focus attention on music cultures. In most, even vaguely academic discussions about pop music, something is made of the vitality of the culture, its grass-roots quality, it 'lived-in-ness', its distance and distancing from high-taste culture. While there is an element of truth here of course, the relationship between the given and the adopted/adapted should not be been as unproblematic.

Firstly, there is the question of the material of life upon which people 'work', *i.e.*, what is it that people are socialised into (given issues of adaptation, mediation, *etc.*). What/where is the point from which they 'start' to use the culture, turning it into their own culture? This is true for individuals and social groups, especially where the latter see themselves as music/cultural groups.

Of course the lived and living tradition within popular culture is seen as of great importance. Each new generation, in that place, or that class, or that sex, or that ethnic, religious group *etc.*, 'takes on' the past in both senses of take on. However, what must not be overlooked or taken for granted is what economic /commercial, political/cultural forces, influences, were present, at play, dominant, significant, *etc.*, at the time? Because, besides anything else, we should ask ourselves, "How different would it be now, if it had been different then?" Or, "If social, cultural developments had taken a particular course then, rather than the one they did, where might we be going now?"; and most significantly, "What were the specific *and* general cultural influences at that time, in the place, *etc.*, that helped to form people's attitudes?" and so on, that would lead them to (expect) accept or reject, tolerate or react against this or that course of social development or information about social facts.

The extant conventions of youth and music culture are an aspect of the relationship between character and social structure. What is regarded as good and bad, acceptable or not, questions of aesthetic values, are crucial. Take, for example, the convention of 'hot' and 'cool'. One of the enduring qualities of Rock 'n' Roll culture in the 1950s and early '60s have kept an association going, but, in the main, it has led to the development of 'Rock music and Rock culture', which, while not being ideologically of the establishment, is usually 'Cool', detached, sardonic, *etc.*

85

It is one of the qualities of successive generations of young persons and their role in the development of music related cultures that they relocate the 'hot' values into what they are doing. The form may be different of course, the content certainly will vary, but the essential purpose remains the same.

"What're you rebelling against, Johnny?"
"Whaddya got?"

This aspect of the relation between youth and music is reflected in the argument that youth music cultures are either a radical answer to, or a blissful escape from, the realities of life. Equally, this view is argued as liberation versus domestication of youth prospects. Whatever we call this debate, these views expressed above are just too simplistic an account. There is inevitably a double edge to these prospects. From romance and 'lover's rock' at one end of the spectrum, to radical intellectualism at the other, there are endless possibilities for variations on a theme. Musical cultures are not only a way of life; they are for the vast majority of young persons a fact of life. Just as much a fact of life as class variable on the one hand, to delinquency prone situations or the likely withdrawal of the commitment to conformity on the other. Indeed the process of responses to the pressures for conformity or nonconformity given by the musical culture 'space' may well have allowed young people in the UK to 'negotiate' a place. There have been many accounts of these 'negotiations', for essentially this theory suggests that young people are neither 'fish nor foul' - they can and do cope given a little bit of help from their friends. Most young people, of whatever generation or class, seem likely to support, replicate and legitimate the dominant order. However, it has always seemed more important that a very significant section of post-war upper working class and middle class youth have replicated in their own terms, a situation of peaceful co-existence with the dominant order. Those generations of post 11+ grammar school pupils in the late 1940s to mid-1960s seem a good example. Many pupils went to the grammar schools and found themselves in an unfamiliar setting to say the least. What they needed to do perhaps was to work out or negotiate a position within that system that was tolerable and still allowed them to be *without* the system. This enabled them to hang on to Elvis and Buddy, the Everleys, Chuck Berry, Muddy Waters, Lonni Donnigan and Cliff, while still being part of all that elbow-patches and Gilbert and Sullivan stuff.

I would argue that, within this negotiated space, then and now, it is the musical structuring and the social and self-manifestations of self-expression that really stands out as a dynamic and invigorating accompaniment to, and antidote for, everyday life. One of the more quixotic characteristics of the youth music relation is that so much private venture, experiment and experience became public property, often in ways that ranged from just surprising to embarrassing.

It is also appropriate to mention the centrality of ritual and celebration in relation to the public and private issue. The experience of all cultures is to create *music* to perform ritual and celebratory functions. It is also true for the development of music for contemplation and emotional experience. What is evident for youth culture development is that this is all true in varying degree. What is also interesting is the revolt into style and/or style into revolt aspect of this culture generality.

It is commonplace, within post-war sociology, to encounter the 'over socialised conception of man' debate. I have already suggested that the relationship between character and social structure, the concept of the sociological imagination and the problem of social control and action are relevant aspects of a discussion about youth and music cultures. The 'over-socialised' debate further underlines the dangers that have and still do exist in arguing for a causal alchemy in the development of youth and music cultures. We know enough about the development of *music* and about the development of age-specific groupings to argue that there may well be an 'environmental' association between youth and music styles and class or life choices and chances or gender, or race; but there is no necessity about it. This is not to deny that these associations do exist, that there might be a 'dole queue rock' for example; for that particular music or this particular style, may have its origins elsewhere, its reasons various, its antecedents obscure, its effects both latent and manifest.

Towards a conclusion let me develop a little further some key theoretical/ideological issues. I am very cautious about what can be said about youth and music cultures from the 'outside' of those cultures, even if this is a sociological 'outside'. This is not to say that we should not try, as I do believe that sociology can take us forward and can act as a counter to the dangers of endless self-referential explanations that come from the youth-music 'inside'. I am also most certainly aware that sociology is one of the creations of modernity that still vigorously asserts that the transformations of our age are the birth pangs of a better life.

It is dangerous to make generalisations and yet it is equally difficult to select examples that can be truly representative. After all, a way of seeing is also a way of not seeing something else. I am also very conscious of the politics of studying youth-music cultures, in the sense here that people offering an account of musical phenomenon do offer a politics of doing it, whether that is made explicit or not. Let me suggest one key aspect of this.

One (or the most?) important intellectual battle-ground has been the one on which the struggles about relative autonomy have taken place. Most sociological accounts of pop music (and other pop cultures like TV) have emphasised that the pop product stems from a set of social relations that at least in capitalism are part of commercial interests. The economic base of ownership and control of the pop industry is the first 'port of call' in understanding why the cultural product *is like it is*.

The product, consumed by a mass 'audience', also carries crucial ideological features that not only reproduce the desire for the pop product *as it is*, but also for the set of socio-economic relations of production-consumption *as they are*.

What also happens, of course, is a reproduction and relegitimation socially, via culturally, of other social relations such as gender, race, age, knowledge transmission orthodoxies, *etc*. Before long we end up with an analysis of the materialist *basis* of people's lives, socio-economic *practices* and the production and reproduction of *ideas*. This explanation is based fairly explicitly on a particular reading of Marx, incorporating ideas about base and superstructure, false consciousness, *etc*.

This explanation has been very convenient for sociology in recent times (and other social theorising outside of 'sociology'), as it does deal with *fact*, real people's lives and *theory*, the hidden structures of relations, that need to be exposed. However, it is plain to see that there are problems with reductionism here. Does every aspect about the life and times of pop have its genesis in the socio-economic relations of ownership, control and the motivations of the music industry?

A set of alternative explanations has appeared, therefore, which have sought to argue for the relative autonomy of the pop cultures.

In brief, it is suggested that what happens 'within' the socio-cultural relations of pop, including, crucially, the aesthetic concerns, judgements and actions of musicians, audiences and critics, is often invariably, independent of the crasser profit making, status quo reproducing actions of the moguls of the pop-commercial nexus. The *vitality* and self-consciousness of pop keeps it 'shadow-boxing' with the 'nexus'. The consumers of pop are not a docile consuming mass that is mindless of the manipulation that is taking place. These *consumers* are also *producers* of an aesthetic, a socio-cultural musical value that, combined with the sensuous, emotive forms of musical self-expression and perhaps a politics of alternatives and oppositions, offers a considerable dynamic force with which to challenge the very economic base. However, while it is one thing to argue that consumers are active mediators, 'imposing their own' meaning on the products, it is far more problematic to argue that these mediations 'reach' the relations *as well*.

In this discussion, the question of *agency* is refocused. This is also a discussion of post-modernist ideas in that these 'newer' cultural practices transcend the 'older' modernist cultural relations, embodying as the latter did *class* forces and ideological struggles.

Again, it is possible to see how attractive this line of theorising is. However, it can also be seen that there are dangers of offering an *idealist* explanation of pop music (and cultural) phenomenon that are 'free-floating', devoid of any connection with the material conditions of *real* people's lives, the actual socio-economic relations of society and the continued existence of real power struggles of a life and death nature. It should be added that the division being posed between these two positions is redundant anyway. The traditional 'Base and Superstructure' arguments were located in an analysis of manufacturing industrial (capitalist) society. The current micro-chip technology, post-industrial society - which greatly affects the nature of music and the politics of its composition, performance and reception - does, in fact, require us to look again at the socio-economic forces and relations of capitalism.

These 'theoretical' difficulties do not remain at the level of abstract theory; they are related to questions of *political* agency. The set of explanations we choose to grasp the reality that is pop, as a socio-cultural phenomenon, are part and parcel of our political actions, what we feel is appropriate, possible, *etc.*, in terms of social change.

So, yes, pop music has played and does play a significant part in both the giving of structure to life, the conferment of identity, and a way in which people can locate the self and the social. I would like to develop more explanations along the lines of social accountability and selfhood in terms of pop music(s). This will force me into much more discussion about pop music aesthetics, the creation of taste and use cultures. I take it as axiomatic here that by 'creation', I do not just reiterate the important, but fairly commonplace, sociological analyses of how the music industry/commercial nexus 'creates' taste, use and production/consumption cultures. As I have indicated throughout this paper, I want to know much more about the creating done by young people themselves, particularly in regard to the interrelation of aspects of their everyday lives and their socio-cultural practices as both a fact of life and a way of life.

NOTES ON THE TEXT:

1. From the song *Somewhere down the crazy river*, Robbie Robertson, 1987.

2. I am thinking here of Hoggart's *Uses of Literacy* (1960), William's 'Culture and Society' (1958), *etc.*

3. This line has been developed more recently by Seabrook, 'What went wrong?' amongst others.

4. For an excellent exposition of this area, looking at the development of the music industry, *etc.* - see Frith, *Sound Effects* (1983).

5. For an interesting and brief review of this debate see Selden, SOCIOLOGY Vol 14 No. 2, May 1980, p.301.

6. Milan Kundera rates a mention here. *The Book of Laughter and Forgetting* (1978) is particularly good. His recently translated book, *The Unbearable Lightness of Being* (1984) should be essential reading.

7. See, 'Why don't we do it in the Road: The Beatles Phenomenon' (1979), Astley. Also see, 'Youth and Music' (Ed.) Astley (1981) an issue of *Social Science Teacher* (Vol.10, No.5, July 1981) available from ATSS. See also the recent series of music/social studies books (aimed at schools and colleges) edited by Vulliamy and Lee, *Popular Music* (1981).

Transformations: a consideration of the role of Ideological Cultural Apparatuses (ICAs)

1982

In the last forty years there has not been one revolution, an industrial and technological revolution, there have been two; and this second, cultural revolution might be called the revolution of images, words and music. People have learned to process images, words and music too; images, words and music and the thoughts and attitudes they embody. We manufacture entertainment and consolation as we manufacture anything else. Or perhaps, to be more cruel, but realistic, the manufacture of images, words and music is a good deal more efficiently manufactured! Take note of the recently reported fact that Lloyd Webber has pocketed ten million pounds largely as a result of convincing a substantial number of people that they ought to consume his product (the same product masquerading as variety) over and over again.

One sees in the shops ordinary old-fashioned goods, oatmeal, custard, *etc.*, and side by side with it, another kind called Instant. . .(Incidentally, one also sees alongside those, a reconstructed old-fashioned product, the one that healthy and hearty people buy.) Most of our images, words and music, Pop, is instant in a sense that they do not require much mediation by the consumer, merely 'open the packet and heat up or add water'. The images, words and music are easy, familiar, instantly recognisable thoughts; the attitudes are familiar, already agreed upon, instantly acceptable attitudes. If this is correct, can these productions be either *truth or music* worth the title? The truth, as we all know, is as Oscar Wilde put it, "Rarely pure, and never simple". Truth is sometimes almost un-recognisably different from what we expected it to be: is sometimes difficult or, even, impossible to accept. But Pop images, words and music are necessarily mixed up with truth, aren't they? Our truth, truth as we know it; one can almost define Pop music as the union of a wish and a truth, or as a wish modified by a truth. But this instant Pop is a wish reinforced by a cliché, a wish proved by a lie. Instant Pop, whether it is Christmas humbug, or oft repeated girl/boy sentimental treacle, or even more oft repeated, dashed--to-pieces-male ego, tells us that life is not only what we wish it, but also what we think it. The makers and purveyors of such Pop treat us exactly as advertisers traditionally treat the readers of adverts; humour us, flatter our prejudices, pull our strings, show us that they know us for what they take us to be: impressionable, prejudiced, status ridden, ignorant; somewhat weak-minded common-folk.

A survey of post election discussions would indicate that one major task for those opposing Thatcher & Co. is to challenge the (growing) orthodoxy about the kind of society we do and should live in. The arguments on Labour politics and changes in the social/class structure of the UK indicate what sociologists have known for years, namely that the configurations *and* representations of 'class' *have* changed decisively. The growth, re-orientation much more towards the young and development of Popular music(s) in the UK has been an essential aspect of these social and cultural changes. From an analysis of 'post-modern' society and youth, the situation is full of contradictions. Most post-modernist thinking suggests the 'end' of culture - the folk idiom - and statuses and hierarchy based on other criteria . . .Moreover, the focus of debate from the late 1950s in regard to 'Youth', has been to argue precisely for a discrete culture or sub-cultures. I would like to return to this issue later, but for now let me emphasise the central significance of analysing 'musical' representations of these social-structural transformations.

In most even vaguely academic discussions about Pop culture, something is made of the vitality of the culture, its grass-roots quality, its 'lived-in-ness', and its distance and distancing from high-taste culture. While there is an element of truth here of course, the relationship between the given and the adop-ted/adapted should not be seen as unproblematic.

Firstly there is the question of the material of life upon which people 'work', *i.e.*, what is it that people are socialised into? (given issues of adaptation, mediation, *etc.*). What/where is the point from which they 'start' to use the culture, turning it into their own culture?

Of course the lived and living tradition within popular culture is seen as of great importance. Each new generation, in that place, or that class, or that sex, or that ethnic, religious group, *etc.*, *etc.*, 'takes on' the past in both senses of "take on". However, what must not be overlooked or taken for granted is what economic/commercial, political, *etc.*, forces influences, were present, at play, dominant, influential, *etc.*, at the time? Because, besides anything else, we should ask ourselves, "How different would it be now, if it had been different then?" or "If social, cultural developments had taken a particular course then, rather than the one they did, where might we be going now?"; and most significantly, "What were the specific and general cultural influences at that time, in the place, *etc.*, that helped to form people's attitudes?" and so on, that would lead them to (expect) accept or reject, tolerate or react against this or that course of social development or information about social facts?

This is not just being difficult for the sake of rewriting history, it does enable us to seriously focus attention on what alternatives there are before us now and indeed ask, Are alternative modes of development being offered on equal terms?

Of course contemporary popular and pop culture can offer a radical voice (even radical words), can pose difficult questions about what we do and how we do it. But it may also be that the inherent inadequacies of that culture; given the dominant forces in its formation, are going to deform the arguments of now.

In discussing the 'grass roots' nature of popular culture, or in those discussions I have prompted about 'lived-in-ness' we should not overlook the continuous debate within sociology about organic and mechanical development. For example, can we assert that pop has essentially grown from 'inside' from the people, or has it mainly been an imposed, even colonising development, or, would it be nearer the truth to argue that there are both forms of development?

Ironically, perhaps we could argue that where aspects of the popular or pop have become/been self-consciously developed politically, it is somewhat more *rational* in its nature. Perhaps, just to make analysis more difficult, it is not enough to reiterate that pop music has been a radical answer to or/and a blissful escape from reality. Perhaps we also need to consider that pop 'music-ing' is also a radical escape from and/or a blissful answer to the realities of life?

Does society, and the pop system therein, confront us as an entity 'outside' of us? Alternatively, is much of pop an attempt to subvert just such a formulation? How can we explain how persons (particularly perhaps young persons) come to place meanings on pop phenomena? We certainly cannot deny that young persons are 'confronted' by a world that, at one and the same time, has created 'youth' and pop. However, we must say in the same breath that young persons have 'contributed' a great deal to the formulation of these conceptualisations and phenomena. How self-conscious are young persons of this duality? Indeed I would go further, how self-conscious are the present generation that matured in the 1960s aware of their own complicity in these matters? If we are going to talk about grass-roots culture and lived-in-ness, *etc.*, we have to closely examine the pop phenomena of the 1960s say and ask ourselves questions about meanings then, illusions and reality, *etc*. For example, was all that liberality merely an ego trip, bolstering up the dominantly individualist values of our times? Was it another commodity fix?

I feel that it is essential to relate these concerns, so identified, with the project of Habermas, his theory of 'communicative action', or put briefly, practical discourse which is unconstrained (by the dominant hegemony of the ruling elites, *etc*.) and which works towards mutual understanding and the possibility of consensual action.

Habermas, in agreeing with Murcuse that our most basic value judgements are rooted in compassion, in our sense for the suffering of others, goes further towards the notion of the bond of friendship, the sympathetic/empathetic effort to understand the 'other'. This is central to the theory of 'communicative action' and may depend on an act of faith, even of life. The aesthetic criteria associated with pop music at its most radical, reflects the vision of wholeness, of the human condition and nature in harmony.

Can culture, can pop culture, be the antithesis of alienation? Is culture working against being lost, powerless, estranged? Does culture, does pop culture, put the *human* person and essentially human action, back in charge?

Perhaps this is against all the odds, natural or social/(commercial) forces? In this context, is pop/can it be, a vision of an alternative future, albeit a utopian one? Can it ever be more than a guide for a journey without 'end'?

Sociology and sociologists are concerned with truth and true understanding of social reality. It would seem that most sociologists join in the quest for the 'Good Society'. To pursue this goal, sociologists seek ideal communication amongst themselves in order that through debate and argument they may reach consensus. It is also evident that sociologists would hope that this practice was more widely used in society in general. If it was, of course, the 'need' for sociologists as such, might wither away, communal life would promote understanding and agreement.

If we feel and believe that the culture industries stand in the way of social transformation, what are we to do about it?

The question of agency must become a (the) central focus for us here. The agency of the Culture Industries, as institutions in society, the agency of the entrepreneurs, bureaucrats and professionals that 'make them up', and the agency of the (predominantly) consumers. The entertainments, *etc.*, agents with their liberal petit-bourgeois values operate with what Stuart Hall has called a linguistic ventriloquism, the forms of media-speak where those exalted elite values are seemingly coming from the mouths of working people; often, as a consequence, denying their actual materialist 'base' and history. This is indeed part of the populism of our time, just as it has been in the past, particularly at the turn of the century in a period of determined imperialism abroad and enthusiastic colonisation of the working class at home.

The role of the Culture Industries is constantly a part of the re-reforming of 'the masses', which is attempted, often with the excuse given that this is what the people want. This is not just an issue of false consciousness, that the masses are culturally stupefied and will, as a consequence, accept anything fed to them, endless 'Bread and Circuses' diet, but that working people do not have, as yet, the tools (nor the inclination/leadership?) or Culture/Media elite corp. This not only raises questions about hegemony and the active struggle against the forces that form and maintain the processes whereby selective reinforcement of certain values directly aids the cultural reproduction that underpins the status quo. Quite literally we are looking at the situation where working people need to formulate what C. Wright Mills and Hans Gerth called a, 'Vocabulary of Motives', *i.e.*, the means whereby they can speak in a reflexive way about their experiences and offer up arguments for alternative futures, in striking contrast to the ones put forward so authoritatively via the media/culture industries.

This should also make us consider by what/through what processes does the Cultural come to have a value upon it? Certainly one aspect of this is that higher and lower values, exalted and dethroned, dominant and subordinate relations are represented through most of the products of the Culture Industries and most certainly through most of Pop. This represents, of course, the dominating form and structures of an undemocratic (indeed actively anti-democratic), capitalist structure of social relations. In other words, Pop has consistently been 'used' to reinforce, through reemphasis, what there is. This is an example of what I would call the work of the Ideological Cultural Apparatuses (ICAs).

However, what also needs to be taken into consideration here is the constantly occurring struggle on the fringes and margins, the footnotes, of Pop. This struggle, both form and content as well as purpose, argues precisely the question of what values should be presented, promoted championed, *etc.* It also argues over, and through, what kind of representation of the life experience of the subordinated should be offered up to them via the Culture Industries. To what degree and in what way can/should the 'sub-text' of those lives be used to express what is hidden from view, deliberately or accidentally. The labour/socialist movement has to orientate itself to some fundamental issues here. How does the socialising and social control processes actually seem to work on people? Why (or not) are they effective in the influencing of ideas and actions? How might these apparatuses be used to raise and develop ideas that are different, alternative and critical? This requires a good deal of imagination to formulate approaches both recognisable and challenging. While this reorientation of the role of the Culture Industries must relate to questions of material acquisition of deprived and disadvantaged people, *i.e.*, a substantial improvement in their real standard of living; it does and must, relate to a reassessment of roles and relationships, gender, race, age, *etc.* As an ideological sign, Pop is replete with contradictions about its origins, its function, its purpose, *etc.* It is certainly largely formed by the contending class interests and values that have been, and are, brought to it daily, in the struggles I have already indicated. The struggles that take place (past and present) on the 'site' of Pop both represent and produce wider issues of social change. However, it is quite clear that the agents of the ICAs are constantly, earnestly engaged in their attempt to deprive this sign of this particular significance. They do all they can, and are successful by degrees from time to time, to 'neuter' this sign, to render it impotent, or to make us believe that it is not potentially or actually a vehicle for change. There has always been this 'double state' to Popular and Pop Culture, *containment and resistance*; the radical answer to and the blissful escape from the realities of life. What we have seen in recent years when a certain decadent chic indifference has entered into Pop more and more is the 'radical' escape from, blissful answer to, the realities of life. This high-tech cleverness and apologia for privilege maintenance in the face of 'all the odds' should be challenged by those who are concerned about bringing about some significant social changes in this society.

I am suggesting, therefore, that to be able to make progress in these matters we need to: (a) understand the nature of the culture industries and their effect on people, ideas and actions; and, (b) debate how we might use these apparatus for social change. ICAs are a key here, let me suggest why. Firstly, what am I trying to get at, to study? What aspect of the production, reproduction and significance of Culture am I attempting to observe, analyse and understand? I feel this is important because I want to be as precise as possible about the area, or field of my concern. It is some aspects of the distinctiveness of the Cultural Field, practices and struggles, which I see worthy of separate study.

1. All these practices whose principal function is significant.
2. The institutions that organise them; and
3. The agents that operate them.

All three of these concerns are intimately linked to my concept of ICAs.

This approach would encompass challenges to particular representations or orders of representation and other issues like the nature of the context of relations, internal and external of the Institutions of Cultural significance; the Media and the agencies of Popular and Pop Culture in general. The relation of such Institutions and Institutional practices to the State and to Capital and Labour would also be significant. Part of any general concern of mine about these Institutions and their practices would be the question of differential accessibility to the means of cultural production; what opportunities do minority, alternative or oppositional groups or movements have?

What is the likely nature of their practice when they do gain access, albeit limited and circumscribed? For example, let me pose three questions (and a rider) about Pop.

1. Is pop music trying to pose an alternative set of values to the dominant ones in our society associated with and supportive of capitalism?
2. If the answer to this is yes (even in part), is pop music, culture, the musicians, *etc.*, any good at it?
3. Is it possible to use what sociological theories have been developed about an 'ideal communication', from Mills to Habermas, to more clearly comprehend how Pop might pose real alternatives? This would certainly involve a discussion of the relation 'between' alienation and post-modernism as crucial concepts at the heart of a heartless world.

Taking these together, it raises a fundamental question in my mind.

One of the issues I find of interest here is the question of adoption. In what ways, and through what processes, do certain ideologies come to be adopted by people, classes, *etc*? This brings me back to the question of grassroots-ness discussed earlier, but re-orientates the focus of questions to 'media' culture production: as a process, and the production of 'culture(s)' with all the attendant and recognisable artefacts, customs and practices, *etc.*

One of the reasons for me that the Institutions of the Media, of Popular Culture, are of crucial concern is then related to my working notion of Culture having to do with production. I see cultural products as practices in terms of the relations between their material conditions of existence and their work as representations that produce meanings. I take a 'formalist' rather than a 'realist' approach here in that I do see the ICAs as directly engaged, with differing degrees of self-consciousness, in the process of production. I am, therefore, concerned with the modes of production and with modes of signification.

In other words, the Media is not 'merely' a 'window' or a 'mirror' of reality, which may or may not be ideological, but is actually engaged in the production of 'reality'.

I am well aware of the problems that this approach brings with it. For example, what am I to make of the 'obvious' differences in the production of the objects or services usually associated with the role of manufacturing or service industry and the nature of that consumption, the conventional wisdoms and day-to-day routines of people's lives associated with it? Am I to say that the 'goods' and 'services' produced by the manufacturers or producers of Culture are the same in essence? If this is even in part true, can I then use the same analytical tools to discuss these production processes, the nature and relations of consumption and so on, *as alienation*, or these practices as alienating?

I am aware of the realm of problems raised by Marcuse: "With the affirmation of the inwardness of subjectivity, the individual steps out of the network of exchange relationships and exchange values, withdraws from the reality of bourgeois society, and enters another dimension of existence. Indeed this escape from reality led to an experience which could (and did) become a powerful force in invalidating the actually prevailing bourgeois values, namely, by shifting the focus of individuals' realisation from the domain of the performance principle and the profit motive to that of the inner resources of the human being: passion, imagination, conscience. Moreover, withdrawal and retreat were not the last position. Subjectivity strove to break out of its inwardness into the material and intellectual culture." (Marcuse, *The Aesthetic Dimension*).

What I would want to do is to be able to relocate these questions in the 'mainstream' of sociological discourse about production, consumption, the forces and relations thereof, and alienation. Let me attempt a few tentative suggestions.

Much has been written recently about our 'present' cultural state of post-modernity. This has, in fact, been argued by some sociologists about industrialism, capitalism, statism, legitimisation crisis, *etc.*, in society in general. So in some ways the culture/aesthetics arguments about the ending/death of modernism and the nature. . .possible, probable, *etc.*, of post-modernism has at least been *pre*-dated by a more general socio-political critique of change in the latter part of this century.

This should, and I think it does, make us reflect on the generation that preceded this 'traumatic change'. The stresses and strains of post-war industrial urban life are, of course, reflected in the 'products' of that era.

(But not just, of course, in any simple reductionist way, *i.e.*, we still have to take into account the relative autonomy of cultural 'products'). This is certainly true of pop-culture products. If modern/late capitalism has created a society and culture dominated by individualism, hedonism, acquisitiveness and consumption, has this added to the rifts between people, as individuals or groups or classes, *etc.*, as collective entities of this phenomenon?

If alienation is a key concept to use in considering the nature and condition of society today, are we saying that the rifts are so great/structural, *etc.* that the very notion of 'society' has been put in question, the outcome of events in some doubt?

So, what is the manifestation of these phenomena of Popular culture? Particularly with reference to the late 1950s' is, for example, the Rock 'n' Roll culture the antithesis of all this 'lonely crowd', 'organisation man' alienation stuff?

The debate on the politics of pleasure seems to be raising questions about mass culture and ideology in terms of pop as false needs/false consciousness.

There has always been a significant split between 'mainstream', overtly commercial pop and the intellectualised, arty forms. It may be that this latter form is a manifestation of the wider 'alienation-ish' social critique of society and culture? If this is so, or even a partial truth, has any of this been changed by our movement into the post-modernist phase?

A thought . . . was punk the modernist watershed of post-war pop music/culture?

Popular culture in general and, in particular, popular music, is in many ways dominated by the present (albeit with the usual reservations about any cultural form not just being about now). It is the immediate that matters, through which the past is seen darkly in varying degrees of haziness and nostalgia.

One major aspect of the post-modern theory (*e.g.,* Bell and Riesman . . .although he recanted later) was the assumption of an economy and culture of abundance, a culture dominated by consumption and self-conscious consuming with all the issues of style *etc.*, that go with that (*e.g.,* Pop Art as a movement fed very heavily on this and in terms of cultural critique brought it to the fore).

It is true that part of this assumed abundance in the UK came via the values and actual provisions of the Welfare State.

On both sides of the Atlantic (and later in Japan, *etc.*) the theory of abundance did have its critics, even, and in terms of what I am arguing, particularly at the height of its popularity, which, of course, for most people, manifested itself wrapped up in a popular-psychology of progress, being modern, contemporary, *etc.*

One of the most interesting expressions of this critique in the USA was Jarrell's 'A sad heart at the supermarket' where, with heavy irony, he 'collapses' the production of food with the production of culture.

So again, what is pertinent here, is what of this debate resonates through popular culture in general and through Pop? Has the punk, post-punk era signalled an end, a loss of belief in, or even an actual empirical end of, the era of abundance? If this is true (and it would be easy to cite numerous examples of such a social critique through youth-based music cultures in the 70s and 80s), what about the continued and continual outpourings of the great majority of pop? Is this to be seen as more veneer, more 'gliding the ghetto', more false consciousness hedonism?

The continued and very profitable existence of 'Rock' music is, in itself, an indication of how a generation, the generation that were the 'youth' in the late 50s and 60s, have no intention of giving up their view of, or beliefs in, that era. So the 'Rock culture producers' go on turning out the goodies for the ageing consumers, which, of course, in the main, offers little or no threat to their thinking, or lack of it. But even these sales are going down as signalled by the recent BPI campaign, 'Life goes better to music'. One of the reasons why some people in their late 30s and 40s have such difficulty in understanding most young people's lives and problems is because they, the oldies, still believe in the ideas of an economy, society and culture(s) of abundance, opportunity, *etc.*, or hold on to beliefs about social roles and relationships that echo their past.

At this point, it may be useful to turn our attention towards the specific 'youth' dimensions of the issue. This might be particularly important if we are to embrace the notion that the young might, actually or potentially, be in the vanguard of social change. The relationship between youth and music seems, from a distance, in sharp enough focus. When we get up-close, things, understandably perhaps, look differently. Not just in the sense of where the focus might be, but also that what becomes sharp and diffuse or blurred can change alarmingly. Illusion and reality.

The artefact of pop culture is, by definition, on the surface of life; however, what has generated it/formed it/caused it to come about, is far from skin deep. The lives that pop seems to mirror, mimic, from (in part), express or represent are, in fact, what really matters. It is this that is really interesting, formidable and significant for the sociologist. This is not to say that the products of the pop process are not important and vital in (and does) take us through an amazing spectrum of the sublime to the ridiculous. Non-pop, elite-cultural products, are very weighty matters in contrast, laden down with content significance, but it is, in the main, an 'inherited' culture; it is part of the property, the cultural capital, that is passed on from one generation elite to the next. With few exceptions, it remains a received culture, it is, unlike pop, not much concerned with the process, 'the journey', more concerned with the end product and its value-laden place in the constellation of acceptable mores of everyday life. What is also of interest here is the conviction among many socialists today that any cultural-aesthetic challenge to ruling elites hegemony must start from an elitist, indeed avant-garde position. What I understand is meant by this is that it is no longer appropriate (if it ever was) to 'use' pop - the supposedly youthful and accessible culture - to promote socialist ideas and strategies.

To what extent has the development of pop music, since the war, really been a product of a young person's activity and/or commercial exploitation? To what extent have young persons been diverted from their commitment to conformity, or become conformists, as a result of their engagement with these musical phenomena? To what extent have policy makers, practitioners of institutional and administrative values seen the development of youth and music cultures as a threat, diversion, *etc*? It is that musical activity and associations are the social form, the most commonplace way, that young persons can create some space for themselves in their complex network of relations? It is worth reminding ourselves of another sociological conventional wisdom here, namely the assumed interrelation between socialisation, social control and social order. It is commonplace to argue that the young, in particular, find themselves influenced and constrained by the various dominating social institutions of our society.

What young people are likely to experience may not be as arbitrary as what they seem to do. The sense in which the impulse of the moment, the spontaneous expression, may become the byword of a social category, is important in understanding youth. So much of the everyday lives of the young now, and in the 1950s/60s, is set within a framework of typicality and likelihood. Family, neighbourhood, peers, school, youth clubs, law and order, media, workplace, romance, *etc.* These and other aspects of a young person's life both liberate and circumscribe, domesticate. Youth are not simply or merely the carriers of existing culture. Nor are they just the inheritors of custom and practice. It would also be wrong to suggest that they face existing, perhaps dominating, cultures (including institutional cultures) and have to absorb that culture, those social roles, as part of their socialising. The accumulation of knowledge of ways of life is more complex than that. We are all, young and old, seekers of social knowledge *and* knowledge.

Pop, like the individual, offers theories of the world in abundance. How satisfactory they are, or how well we, or Pop, may articulate them is another matter. How do the young get to know about the adult roles they will adopt, reject or modify? These roles must exist independently of youth actually experiencing them *as a person.* What we have here is what might be described as a vocabulary of motives. Young people have motives imputed to them; they impute motives to others and themselves. Pop music is a symbol system used by all and sundry, not just as pleasure, leisure, politics, religion, *etc.*, but also used as a 'battleground' of the imputing of motives for actions. How are ideas about roles, choices, life, *etc.*, to be communicated? What is quite evident is that for good or for ill, pop music is used by all manner of people to convey ideas about what life is like, was like, and should be like.

One example of the problems here is the complementary undercurrents of cultural diversity, consensus and/or conflict over time. It is true to say that we can trace the development of the interrelation of youth and music cultures, say, over the last four decades. But can we argue that it is possible to compare, and thereby evaluate, what is happening now with what was happening then? I think not. The picture becomes even more cluttered if we consider the role of social policy in the years since the war. No doubt the policy makers did start out with some fixed, conservative notions about the place and role of young persons in society after the war. Surprisingly enough, though, the policy makers, concerned primarily with youth policy, were very aware of the *changed circumstances* that had come to exist in the post-war 'space' and as a part of the post-war 'settlement'. Take, for example, the problem of sociology's response to the post-war trans-Atlantic world. I have always felt that the tension created by the structural-functionalist grand theorising on the one hand and the pragmatic humanism on the other hand, has been one of the most fascinating aspects of the development of sociology in the 1950s. One of the key aspects of this pragmatic humanist critique of society was a concern with alienation. This alienation was seen as part and parcel of the stresses and strains of post-war western life. The rifts between social and human needs and the dominating relations of the day seemed so great that the very future of society *and* the mental stability of the person were in question. Of course the pragmatic humanist movement and moment was mainly in America. However, to whatever side of the Atlantic we look, what has interested me in respect to the youth and pop music culture in particular is, How did alienation phenomenon come to be represented in post-war pop? At the heart of the pragmatic humanist critique of post-war society is a series of questions which focus upon 'abundance for what', the nature of the 'organisation man' and the 'lonely crowd', linked in many cases with an exploration of imagination and its possible liberating role. These questions conjure up the spectre of the alienated human at odds with society. Here is a view of the modern person, old and young, symbolically dislocated, seemingly torn out of the context of the social institutions of which she/he depends. Self and institutional order no longer mesh. This has innumerable resonances in the discussions about the politics of pleasure, the 'doped mass', the mass culture and the commodification of creativity.

The out-pouring of pop from the 1950s seems to be the very antithesis of this humanist critique most of the time. It is voguish now to speak of youth in the 1980s as the 'lost generation'. Can we, therefore, assume that in using this idea, some comparison is being made with the past, with a 'found generation' perhaps? The precarious liberty and liberality of the 1960s was experienced and shared in the most part by the immediate post-war generation. The intra- and post-war reconstruction of society was not just a bricks and mortar job, it was, besides everything else, a reconstruction of cultures and values. It is, as I have already indicated, significant that most of the policy making is stronger and indeed was rooted first and foremost in the dominant and dominating institutional values of the 1940s and 1950s. From the young person's point of view, the decade and a half after the war was a peculiar mish-mash of excursions and alarms. There appears, perhaps more so with hindsight, to have been a path of social and cultural development to follow, but in fact, life was more maze-like than anything else.

There are inevitably many ifs and buts here. If post-war British society had not moved towards a welfare state on the one hand and an increasing consumer led economic expansion on the other, would young people have had what scope they did? If numerous forms of American popular culture had not penetrated UK air space so soon, would there have been the increasingly precocious musical development here? If the collective warfare to welfare spirit had not prevailed, would there have been so much for the young to have and be resented for?

There can be little doubt that the economic and socio-political developments that took place after 1942, say, created a degree of 'space' that allowed the formation of a post-war generation of 'youth' plus the associated enthusiasm, creation, mediation, adoption, *etc.*, of distinctive looking and sounding cultures. And again it should be noted that commerce was engaged in both opening up this 'space' and 'pushing back the frontier' and engaged in filling this space with artefacts. So it could be argued that the post-war generation were 'found' in possession of much lethal equipment with which to perpetrate their grotesque and dastardly deeds up to and including the 1960s. The post-war generation's *direct* affect on youth and music cultures came to an end in the mid-ish 1960s. From that point the starting place for much of the interrelation between youth and music shifted to another site. This is not to say that the traditions, some important values, cultural patterns, *etc.*, of the post-war scene were completely thrown out; far from it. They were, in a residual culture sense, relocated within the aspects of emergent pop, youth and music cultures seemed to undermine the classless nature of British society. We know of course, that this is not strictly true. We have experienced the American phenomenon for treating stratification as an issue of occupationally led status ranking. This view, there and here, placed great emphasis on liberality, affluence, consensus and embourgeoisement. This is not to say that class did not figure in the assessments of social and cultural development on both sides of the Atlantic; it did, but the focus had turned away from conflict.

In the UK, the most interesting writing on class formation, consciousness and cultures was being written 'outside' of sociology to a great extent. A good deal of emphasis was being placed on the changing circumstances of the working class, focusing particularly interestingly from the point of view, on the crisis of working class hegemony, or the cultural imperialism of the middle and entrepreneurial classes. There is an undercurrent in much of this writing (particularly in the 1950s and early 1960s) which suggests that the working class - and even more so(?)

their political leaders - colluded in their own cultural subordination. There is a sense here that the educational values of the 1950s and early 1960s, for example, inadequately prepared the working class for the problems that lay ahead. There are echoes here of the timeless radical demand for an education to create/provide 'really useful knowledge'. But the lesser of these issues was the question of non-work time and ways in which the young (working class males in the main) might develop leisure activities in a part response to their newly 'found' status in society.

What is particularly important here is the detail of the relationship between the young and leisure. It seems immaterial what point of the 1950s-80s is considered, because what can be seen is an extremely complicated network of interrelations between young persons, their families, neighbourhoods, schools, workplaces, leisure-time places, the media in general - and the music industry in particular. Of course what the 'surface' looks like at any one time is greatly affected by fads and fashions, but it is also affected by the processes that formed and reforms post-war popular and pop culture. I do not have any doubts about the relative autonomy of much of popular and pop culture over the last thirty years or so. Indeed, one of the more interesting aspects of this phenomenon is the relation between fact and fiction in any writing about these years.

An important (and currently very notable) aspect of much of the best fiction writing over the post-war years - prose, essays, poetry, films, *etc.* - is to use, intersperse in the texts, 'extracts from real life'. This takes many forms of history; texts, documentary, visual images, sounds and so on. However, it should be remembered that this 'real history' (in whatever form) is, in fact, constructed or manufactured; selected, edited, deliberately formed through juxtaposition, compassion and so on. In short, it has an ideology. It has also been formed under certain sets of circumstances for certain purposes, using, as often as not, conventionalised, often 'transparent', means of doing so. This juxtaposition of fact and fiction is not only significant in terms of its appearance together, but also in the assumption of 'writer and reader' about the nature of the *parts and the whole*. Take any example of the rise to fame and fortune of a pop band/musician of the 50s or 60s onwards. 'Beatlemania' is , by definition, a testimony to the significance of story telling in the formation of reality. If we look at films like, *That'll be the Day*, it is inevitable that fact or fiction will overlap and so on, even more so *A Hard Day's Night*. More and more, life imitates art.

In the kaleidoscopic formation of any popular or pop culture to do with youth, the tellings and retelling matters a great deal. It not only exists among the users, focus and so on, it gets replanted within the very music culture itself. In all the business of action and reaction, signs and symbols, it is not just what people say, do, write, or sing that matters, it is also whether people believe it; how does it make them feel and act?

The extant conventions of youth and music culture are an aspect of the relationship between character and social structure. In what is regarded as good or bad, acceptable or not, questions of aesthetic values are crucial. Take for example the convention of 'hot' and 'cool'. One of the enduring qualities of Rock 'n' Roll is that it is hot, *i.e.*, it is edgy, recalcitrant and sexual. A good many young people associated with Rock 'n' Roll culture in the 1950s and early 60s have kept an association going, but, in the main, it has led to the development of 'Rock music and Rock culture', which, while not being ideologically of the establishment, is usually, 'cool'.

It is one of the qualities of successive generations of young persons and their role in the development of music-related cultures that they relocate the 'hot' values into what they are doing. The form may be different; of course, the content certainly will vary, but the essential purpose remains the same.

"What 're you rebelling against, Johnny?"
"Whaddya got?"

This aspect of the relation between youth and music is reflected in the argument that youth music cultures are either a radical answer to, or a blissful escape from, the realities of life. Equally, this view is argued as liberation versus domestication of youth prospect. Whatever we call this debate, these views expressed above are just too simplistic an account. There is inevitably a double edge to these prospects. From romance and 'lover's rock' at one end of the spectrum to radical intellectualism at the other, there are endless possibilities for variations on a theme. Musical phenomenon are not only a way of life, they are for the vast majority of young persons, a fact of life. Just as much a fact of life as class variables on the one hand, to delinquency prone situations or the likely withdrawal of the commitment to conformity on the other. Indeed, the process of responses to the pressures for conformity or non-conformity given by the musical culture, 'space', may well have allowed young people in the UK to 'negotiate' a place.

There have been several accounts of this 'negotiation' business, for essentially this theory suggests that young people are neither 'fish nor fowl' - they can and do cope given "a little bit of help from their friends". Most young people, of whatever generation or class, seem likely to support, replicate and legitimate the dominant order. However, it has always seemed more important to note that a very significant section of post-war upper working class and middle class youth have replicated in there own terms, a situation of peaceful co-existence with the dominant order. Those generations of post 11+ grammar school pupils in the late 1940s to mid-1960s seem a good example. Many pupils went to the grammar schools and found themselves in an unfamiliar setting to say the least. What they needed to do perhaps was to work out or negotiate a position within that system that was tolerable *and* still allowed them to be *without* the system. This enabled them to hang on to Elvis and Buddy, the Everleys, Chuck Berry, Muddy Waters, Lonni Donnigan and Cliff, while still maintaining a tenuous relationship with all the elbow-patches and Gilbert and Sullivan stuff.

I would argue that within this negotiated space, then and now, it is the musical manifestations of self-expression, this cultural praxis, which really stands out as a dynamic and invigorating accompaniment to, and antidote, for everyday life. One of the more quixotic characteristics of the youth music relation is that so much private venture, experiment and experience became public property, often in ways that ranged from just surprising to embarrassing.

It is also appropriate to mention the centrality of ritual and celebration in relation to the public and private issue. The experience of all cultures is to create music to perform ritual and celebratory functions. It is also true, for the development of *music*, for contemplation and emotional experience.

What is evident for youth culture development is that this is all true in varying degrees. What is also interesting is the revolt into style and/or style into revolt aspect of this culture generality.

It is commonplace, within post-war sociology, to encounter the 'over socialised conception of man' debate. I have already suggested that the relationship between character and social structure, the concept of the sociological imagination and the problem of social control and action are relevant aspects of a discussion about youth and music cultures. The 'over-socialised' debate further underlines the dangers that have and still do exist in arguing for a casual alchemy in the development of youth and music cultures. We know enough about the development of *music* and about the development of age-specific grouping to argue that there may well be an 'environmental' or 'anthropological' association between youth and music styles and class or life choices, or gender, or race; but there is no necessity about it. This is not to deny that these associations do exist, that there might be a 'dole queue rock' for example; for *that* particular music or *this* particular style, may have its origins elsewhere, its reasons various, its antecedents obscure, its effects both latent and manifest.

Youth policy and the micro-politics of professional interventions and practices

1988

Politics is about resources. It is about the allocation of resources and the decisions that are taken about their allocation. It is about the power to make decisions about allocation. It is about how power comes to be more the province of some individuals and social groups than of others, and how this fact affects resources. As social theorists, we are concerned with the social basis of politics, with, for example, how it is that some individuals or groups come to have more decision making and power than others? What is the history of these unequal relations, what forces are at work, which seek or serve to maintain or change these situations? However, we can no longer just talk in conventional and traditional terms of the individual or of social class. We live in a time of bureaucratic organisations, some of which administer 'welfare'. Even when the government is dramatically changing the role of State Institutions, the influence of these bureaucracies can be felt. Part of this change is an increasing split between bureaucratic and professional motivations, values, means and ends. What follows is an attempt to examine the nature and consequences of this split.

We have, within our welfare institutions, pro-fessional values, roles and personnel that have been brought about by modernising and often humanitarian forces/factors. These institutions are some of the sites of struggle, 'battlegrounds', for certain kinds of social change set against attempts to resist many such changes. We are also centrally concerned with the power these institutions have to make and shape ideas about decisions, about resources and their allocation. We are concerned to understand the relationship between bureaucratic and professional ideas, practice and authority in these institutions, those engaged in the 'service' of young people.

One aspect of our interest and concern in this bureaucratic/professional split is that it was not always so self-consciously evident to the professionals themselves. In the first flush of development, the institutional roles of social welfare provision, in the widest sense, were seen as good and positive - a clear moral posture embracing a set of ideas that reckoned the outcomes of these welfare interventions to be worth the administrative complexities. Less emphasis was placed on the organisational means than on the ends. The bureaucratic and professional were virtually collapsed together. In the last twenty years or so, the administrative process has become much more a significant issue: means have come to be the focus just as much as ends. Now this may be because professionals love to profess. As people have taken on professional roles they have 'fleshed them out' and made them much more 'a thing in themselves'. It might also be to do with a fundamental shift during the 1960s away from *materialist* goals towards *humanist* ones. It is certainly one result of the curtailment of the expansion of service provision since the 'Oil Crisis' of 1973 and the greater emphasis on the allocation of existing resources.

A good deal of post-1950s writing on 'youth' (on both sides of the Atlantic) has suggested that the young have been predominantly role, rather than goal, orientated. The routine and process(es) of their roles 'within' society, what these roles are, whether young people adopt the roles 'prescribed' for them by society or welfare agencies, or adopt them to their own ends, and the questions about how these roles are to be negotiated and acted out with what consequences, came to be crucial.

The spirit of youth, of the age, was focused on process and means. In the post-war era of abundance for most, the question of material deprivation was pushed to the background. Assumptions were made about the security of the existence of abundance, but 'abundance for what?' Material survival and well-being were secured, but what of spiritual survival and well-being - what of the tensions of alienation? The reorientation to humanist goals became incorporated within the creation/development of many professional welfare roles. The idealism of those projects for the 'good society' came to place increasing pressures on the bureaucratic administration of the social welfare provision apparatus. Was it built to stand not only this test of time, but later still to cope with the additional problems created by economic recession and political sea-changes? We think not. However, here we have, in the late 1980s, a vast array of professional roles in welfare and an equally diverse number of persons to occupy them with differing *political* motivations. It may be true that most recruits to these professional roles have not, self-consciously, reflected upon the kind of questions we have posed. But, we suggest, that for many, their reflections upon their own and other people's professional and bureaucratic *social practices* has come to be a source of some disquiet.

It needs to be added here, that the high value placed upon materialist goals in many sections of our societies has always been embraced by a significant number of welfare professionals. The fact that we have experienced a significant re-legitimisation of these materialist values and goals in the last decade or so should come as no great surprise to us. Indeed, what it should do, is to remind us that in the 'two-steps forward and one-step back' processes of social change, we would be foolish indeed to underestimate the power of residual values. In particular, it should make us reflect upon the tenacity of capitalism and liberal democratic values and the limited (no matter how euphoric we were about it at the time) impact of humanistic values and goals on our social structure(s).

This, amongst other things, is what brings us to explore the 'micro-politics of youth'. We are aware of the fact that, in general terms, the young in the UK society do not have the power to be as equally involved as adults in the decision making processes about the allocation of resources.

We can also suggest, fairly uncontroversially, that some young people, because of their race, or sex, or location, or class, or . . .have even less power than the general conventional norm.

How has this situation come about and been maintained? Why is it that young people tend to have less say than adults over resources and their allocation, even over those resources that *directly* affect them? What is the *social* basis of this situation? What role do Welfare Institutions, bureaucrats and professionals alike, play in the past and the present to create, mediate or change these situations?

There is no doubt that there *is* an inequality of status and power between the 'youth' practitioners, professional or non-professional, (and their bureaucratic associates) and their 'clients' in one guise or another. But is this desirable? Are there perfectly good reasons why decision making on resources is not a set of democratic processes? Is it quite acceptable that the dominant knowledge about the young and their needs in society is largely produced by adults with little or no areas of self-determination afforded to the young?

Can we sleep contentedly in the knowledge that we are doing the best we can in the fair, just and reasonable allocation of resources to the young?

Can we, as professionals or bureaucrats, be sure that the basis for the exercise of the power we have is well informed? How do we feel about the prospect of having even more control, more discretionary powers, on certain terms, from the State or employers? How do we feel about entering into certain kinds of reciprocal relations and partnerships that would mean 'giving up' some or most of this power? What about supporting young people's development of the skills, knowledge, feelings, *etc.*, which will enable them to take some of 'our' power?

We are aware of the fact that an aspect of most discussions about politics concerns the question of social order, consensus and public opinion. Somewhere, in most people's thinking, is a notion about equilibrium and/or stability and the problems associated with maintaining it. In many ways, the question of resources and their allocation is associated with this. Even more so perhaps when attention becomes focused on the fairness of justice of judgements being made about how existing resources are to be allocated or how this allocation should change in the future.

So, while most debates about social order focus on consensus, they also reflect the likelihood or otherwise of conflict. Most certainly conflict over the nature of allocation of resources is commonplace in this society at the present, just as it has been in the past.

It needs to be emphasised that, when people, individually or collectively, make resource decisions about 'youth', they do so with a number of factors affecting their judgement. Not the least of these factors are the conventions of their roles within bureaucracies of welfare provision - whether they are bureaucratic role holders or professionals might be a crucial aspect in their judgement.

What insights do youth practitioners have into their agency as welfare professionals or bureaucrats? To what extent are they reflective practitioners? Does it help them or their clients (or their colleagues, *etc.*)? What do they make of their role(s): can they justify their ideas and actions? What can we learn from their reflections upon the roles they occupy and its wider significance for UK society in the 1980s and 1990s?

At this point it might be helpful to sketch in some outline the nature of the Welfare Institutions that give some structure to inter-generation relations. What we would attempt to do is come closer and closer in focusing our attention on the situation in which the people represented in these pages find themselves. On the one hand: the professionals and the bureaucrats with their roles and job essentially orientated to the young in all their kaleidoscopic complexity. On the other hand: their reflection upon the lives of the people they provide 'services' for, young and old, powerful and powerless, *etc.* While a great deal of theorising has been done about 'youth', young people have been leading their lives in the 'site' (sic) of Welfare Institutions and the bureaucrats and professionals that they are composed of. It is true that in more recent times the analytical study of 'youth' and, more particularly, inter- and intra-generation relations has veered away from the exotic to focus on the conventional and commonplace. However, such a judgement by researchers, ethnographers, *etc.*, needs to be tempered with an open-minded recognition that for many young persons, the 'dividing line' between conformity and non-conformity, the mundane and the exotic, the sacred and profane, obscurity and celebrity, is a very thin line indeed. It could in fact be argued, that many young people criss-cross these dividing lines many times for many different reasons. As a consequence of being in one situation or another, in relation to their everyday lives, actions and association with the welfare agents, they are constantly leading existences which are at least partially structured /conditioned/patterned.

It is certainly not the case that all young people have a uniform experience of these Welfare Institutions, bureaucrats and professionals. A minority of the young have a 'bad' experience with a fairly extensive cross-section. And, of course, what has regularly been referred to as the 'Institutional Bandwagon', seems to be particularly the privilege of the deprived and the disadvantaged as well as the 'depraved'. But this is not exclusively or necessarily so, and we must guard against simplistic assessments that suggest that the 'good ones' experience more influence from their family than welfare and *vice versa* for the rule breakers and nonconformists. There are, of course, many ironies here, not the least of which is the perpetuation of ideas that those 'run of the mill' young people that 'keep out of trouble' get the least share of the resources allocated through the agents of Welfare.

Cynics might suggest that access to some expensive labour power and material resources is open to those who break the rules in conventional ways and for whom standardised causal explanations can be applied. This will appeal to everyone's sense of appropriate intervention and legitimates the very existence of such allocations in the first place. The orthodoxies about what kind of intervention is to be professed and acted upon may, and do change; the assumption that this professing should continue to take place, remains.

However, it would be a gross error of judgement to argue that the bureaucratic and professional agency and intervention is necessarily unwarranted, unwanted or ineffective.

We are not suggesting that a focus on the processes of policy making is an innovation in analysis - far from it. However, we are conscious of the fact that many professional practitioners and administrators are not 'reflective practitioners' to the extent that developing an understanding of the policy making, implementation and evaluation processes that inform their work, are at the top of their agenda.

Such a reflection on the split between professional and bureaucratic values in the context of the 'Youth Service' might enable youth workers to make better sense of the many, and often contradictory, pressures and frustrations they feel in their day-to-day work. It might help them to formulate strategies to better achieve their own and young people's objectives. Among other things, it might look at:

1. Resources for full-time and part-time workers equipment, grants, *etc.*, are often distributed according to criteria reflecting bureaucratic values measuring

numbers rather than the needs of young people or the quality of work done with them. Are workers being forced to direct their efforts to getting large quantities of bodies through the doors of youth centres or are they able to do in-depth work with small groups of young people in the greatest need?

2. Why are youth workers' salaries determined by a grading structure, which emphasises at both a national and local level the amount of work done rather than needs of young people? Should the size of 'Establishment' be a crucial determinant of salaries and how is its measurement negotiated?

3. Do structures of management and support encourage workers to facilitate young people gaining greater control over their own lives where this might involve them in challenging the policies and practices of local and national authorities?

4. One of the most important ideologies accepted by youth work professionals concerns the positive valuation of participation/consultation/sharing with young people. However, this is in direct contradiction to the hierarchical nature of bureaucratic decision-making. Youth workers are frequently not only asked to impose decisions on young people, but are also expected to accept policies and practice on which they have had little influence.

5. Another strong belief of most professional youth workers concerns the value of co-operative working with both young people and other professionals. Working 'alongside' others involves a willingness to make

LIBERATION AND DOMESTICATION

compromises to achieve group goals. We cannot order those whose involvement with us is voluntary to do what we want. This way of working is directly opposed by our existence within a bureaucratic hierarchy where we are either instructed to do things we would rather not or prevented from doing things we would like. When the crunch comes, bureaucratic ideology says, 'instruct', but the professional ideology says, 'negotiate'.

The consequences of these, and other contradictions, are many. They include the frustration and alienation of many youth workers, a lack of confidence in management and an inability to do and get support for certain kinds of work. The pressures on those who perceive and articulate the contradictions include lack of promotion, withdrawal of resources and - in extreme cases - lack of employment. One particular consequence concerns the quality of bureaucratic management. Most workers seem to be faced with one of two unhelpful situations. Either they are closely managed within a strong hierarchy, which gives good support, but imposes control, or they have weak management, which allows freedom to the workers, but offers little support for their positive initiatives. The worst situations are where management offers strong control, but little support, or where it tries to impose bureaucratic procedures on those used to professional autonomy.

There are at least four implications of all this for youth workers themselves:

1. We need to come to an understanding of how the clash between professional and bureaucratic values operates in our particular situations. We then need to use this understanding to formulate strategies by which we can further our own and young people's objectives.

2. These strategies must include a local political one. Local bureaucracies are controlled or managed by, or responsive to, local politicians who have their own agenda regarding young people. Whatever their political party, they may share some of the professional values of youth workers and will, at least, have their constituency needs to protect. This has often enabled youth workers to achieve their aims, where these are blocked, by circumventing the bureaucratic structure and using appropriate political processes. This implies that, as a constant feature of our professional work, we seek to understand and influence the local political process. Youth work is political at both a local and national level because it is about resource allocation as well as methods of working.

3. A crucial element of political strategy must be collective action by youth workers through the appropriate trade union(s). Individual workers can only achieve a limited amount on their own and often this will be at the expense of the interests of other workers or groups of young people. Changes in overall youth work resources or policies or bureaucratic processes can best be brought about by workers building strong union branches, which can negotiate with bureaucratic management, take action

to support objectives and influence political decisions. This will be particularly effective where unions act together. Trade union orga-nisation goes along with the professional values of participation and co-operative working, which youth workers often say they hold dear for young people, but ignore for themselves.

4. Youth workers should adopt a conscious strategy of supporting young people themselves learning the skills, knowledge and understandings, and deve-loping the attitudes to be better able to take political action to achieve their own objectives. Whether this is called political or social education or social action work, it is the means by which youth workers can help people to begin to challenge the bureaucratic and political processes determining their life-chances. As a matter of principle, we should be working with young people to effect the distribution of resources affecting them as well as with other professionals, bureaucrats or politicians.

It is ironic that professional cultures emphasise rationality and reason and yet professional practice often fails to be the outcome of rational thought and reasoning. It may well be that some individuals reject rationality, but do they articulate some reasoned and analytical alternative? Perhaps, as they are engaged in the youth policy micro-politics of resources and life-chances, professionals should be doing more thinking about these matters.

Citizenship, education, identity, and the opportunity structure

1992

INTRODUCTION

One central concern for any democratic society is to ensure that each new generation accedes to the rights and responsibilities of citizenship. Much of this concern is associated with the processes that turn children into role taking adults. Will the younger generation take on the mantle of adulthood, play their part in the continuing development of a civilised society, and in large part legitimate the activities of key social and political institutions?

Social science research has consistently pointed to the problematic nature of the transitions that we, as individuals, make into adulthood. Some of the research has indicated the tendency for many young people to become disaffected with the role of institutions like family, education, work and politics. What should be done about this?

It is clear that one crucial aspect of our maturation is a developing sense of identity in two key ways, a personal identity, 'who am I?' and, secondly, a social identity, 'Where do I fit in, what is expected of me?'

The paper that follows develops these concerns and identifies courses of action.

IDENTITY AND THE OPPORTUNITY STRUCTURE

The recent publication of the book *Careers and Identities* marks the first phase of reporting the major findings of the Economic and Social Research Council's (ESRC) 16-19 initiative. The nationwide research programme was launched in 1986 with the aim of providing reliable and up-to-date data on the attitudes, aspirations and careers of young people in Britain.

The research was innovative in that it attempted to link structural *aspects* of young people's lives, like the affects of the labour market, or gender, or ethnicity discrimination, with psychological influences like self-esteem and the formation of a person's identity through social interaction. One of the main themes of the research has been a focus on socialisation processes, and this was spelt out by the projects director, John Bynner, in 1987.

"Socialisation is a difficult term to pin down, embracing, as it does, both outcomes and the processes which give rise to them. To structural sociologists, it is about economic and political outcomes set against societal structures: who ends up doing what and where and what transitions have they experienced in getting there? For the micro sociologist, with an ethnographic perspective, the focus shifts to the inter-actional context, which bestows meanings on particular forms of economic status and political positions: how is the economic and political world represented in such context and how are roles within it entered?

Psychologists set out to unpack the processes surrounding the formation of occupational and political identity and self-efficacy in the individual; what is the relative importance of the different socialising agencies the young person encounters, and how do these shape attitudes and behaviour?" (Bynner, 1987).

There is a very commonplace concern at the centre of the sociological study of youth to do with the *transition* of adolescents into adults. What are the key elements of this transition for any one person? What roles do key social institutions like family, school, media or religion play? What is the relative importance to be attached to our social engagement with friends? How much of everyday life activity is, in fact, not peculiar to us, but shared in many ways with other people in similar situations, with 'shared' values and outlooks? Indeed, to what extent can it be argued that the life-chances of some young people are very similar, clustered around factors to do with their social class, gender, ethnicity, locality, with their culture group?

The following table (*see* Table 1 *over*), taken from Bynner (1987), emphasises the pattern of interrelation between these influences. It is important for sociologists to take note of the 'social-psychological' processes because within our discussions about agency, we need to understand what it is that persons intend to do (self-efficacy) how they explain events in society and their part in this (representation) and how they attribute cause and effect in their lives (attribution).

One major concern of the ESRC 16-19 research that has always concerned me is whether we can, as social scientists, say anything helpful about the influences that certain agents of socialisation (and social control) actually have on young people's lives. Where, for example, do young people go for advice and guidance on the transitions from adolescence to adulthood? How self-consciously planned and budgeted for are the regular interventions that agents make into young people's lives?

TABLE 1:
Core Elements of Socialisation in the Construction of Adolescent Careers (*source: Bynner, 1987*)

STRUCTURAL INFLUENCES	SOCIALISING AGENCIES	SOCIAL PSYCHOLOGICAL PROCESSES	OUTCOMES OF SOCIALISATION
Labour market	Education/ Training	Identity Self-Efficacy	Economic and Political Status
Social Status	Work	Social representation	Behaviour
Age	Family		Understanding
Gender	Leisure (peer group)	Social attribution	Attitude
Race	Mass media		
Physical attribute (*e.g.*, disability)			

For example, what can we say about the relationship between the adulthood aims of the young, what are their aspirations and expectations, in relation to the development of educational, training and career trajectories?

One aspect of changing life-chances that has not been missed by young adults is their increasing dependency on family, friends, voluntary organisations, and state agencies. I put the state last because this is the sector that has both shrunk in terms of services, care and benefits and been the key policy mover in increasing the dependency of the young on others like family. In reality, more and more young people are left to depend on people whose own resources are already stretched to breaking point. This is even true for the more advantaged, educationally successful 15% or so of young people entering H.E. For very many students of elite education, the experience is a fraught one in a period of continual shrinkage of resources of all kinds.

Recent research on 'young entrepreneurs' also emphasises that while there is plenty of 'enterprise culture' rhetoric, the actual *resources* available are very limited. Locally, in Oxfordshire as elsewhere, there is currently a crisis in the lack of training places due mainly to the 'voluntaristic' approach, where government seeks to make fine speeches, but 'wash their hands' of a more interventionist role that would actually improve the condition of the education, training, careers, incomes, grants, *etc.*, infrastructure. (MacDonald and Coffield, 1991).

It is quite clear from recent studies that, for many young people, their ascribed status - the cumulative consequences of their background - has an even greater significance now in time of recession, high unemployment and cuts in public expenditure. On one hand, young people are exhorted to study and work hard, play their part in society, and they can expect to share the benefits of equal citizenship in John Major's 'classless society'! However, the reality for an increasing - not decreasing - number of young people is that their opportunities are less now.

The authors of 'Careers and Identities' identify this as a crucial issue for the future well-being of the young generation.

'Should we be pessimistic about our young people's futures?' Certainly, unless the necessary conditions for modern adult life are set in place, the vagaries of expanding and contracting labour markets - and irrelevant conceptions of family life and independent living will continue to damage and demoralise. In this respect, young people's, 'generally positive evaluation of their own potential and confidence in their futures is their main insurance against the future.' (Banks *et al*, 1992 p.188/9).

Now, while it is welcoming to hear that many young people remain optimistic in the face of turbulent changes in social life, can it be very healthy that coping with constant threats to their identity and expectations is such a continual part of their life? The transition from child to adolescent to adult is difficult enough as it is in a complex society like ours without these added complications. Clearly, many key agents of socialisation, like parents and teachers, feel increasingly 'out of their depth' in trying to provide the best range of opportunities, guidance and support.

Political apathy has been one further area of concern that has emerged from the ESRC and other recent studies. The evidence points clearly to a growing lack of interest by young people in the politics of society. Apathy may, in fact, be the wrong description for most attitudes, indifference or cynicism may be much more appropriate. However, whatever form this takes, the lack of engagement in political discourses and activities by young people *should be* of great concern to a society in the throes of major changes, upheavals and uncertainties.

Young people in general, (there are obviously some notable exceptions) appear to respond passively to the unfolding events of the last decade or so that have greatly affected their life-chances, their opportunities. Most young people have certainly been 'caught up' in the dominant ideologies of individualism, competition and consumerism. It is certainly true that personal identities have been formed within 'guidelines' set by these ideas about how we should see ourselves in relation to the dominant characteristics of society as regularly promoted by those in power. Indeed, one response by many of those working with, and in the interests of the young, has been to find ways to 'empower' youth.

These processes invariably invite young people to assess their opportunities in relation to their aspirations and expectations. This brings together the question of our personal identity - who *we* think we are - with our social identity - the social position or status that we hold in society. If we are dissatisfied with our opportunities we may need to make informed judgements about why we are unhappy.

Are there relational aspects of ourselves as choice-making persons and the social, economic and political structures in which we live that need to be considered *together* if we are to understand more clearly why our life is like it is? Do we also need to consider to what extent this is not peculiar to us as individuals, but an experience shared by many others? In these circumstances, what exactly are we going to do about it? (Clarke and Saunders, 1991). A good deal of recent social policy has been aimed at making 'youth' more aware of their responsibilities as good and well integrated members of society; conformist and acceptable citizens (Astley, 1991). However, the considerable rise in crime and other 'anti-social' behaviour by some young people taken with a degree of disaffection with the dominant norms of society, has left those in power in contemporary Britain with a feeling of unease about the future. It is one thing to have a non-conformist minority of young people, but the State in Britain as elsewhere, is very unhappy about increasingly large numbers of the young 'turning off' from the dominant values of society. Have we reached that situation in Britain yet, or are most young people still prepared to go along with the dominant "us" idea that society does offer them a fair deal, that they do have equal opportunities, that society is not organised as an adult conspiracy to keep them under control, *etc*?

Many of these questions inevitably return us to

seeking an explanatory framework that emphasises the structure - agency debate. Yes, of course all of our lives are influenced, even determined, by aspects of the social structure, not least of which being the nature and range of adult roles to which we gain access, or desire to gain access. However, how much choice, or agency, do we, as persons, actually have in these matters? To what extent are our ideas about our role(s) in society affected by the development of our identity and *vice versa*?

Clearly we live in a modern society that regularly reinforces the ideology of individual freedom of choice and yet the evidence from social scientific research, like the ESRC study, reminds us that, for many young people, their choices are considerably circumscribed by the social structure and that little has changed since their parent's time as young adults.

It is certainly true that society is very much 'at a crossroads' in regard to young people and their socialisation. It is clear that much more emphasis needs to be put on the gathering and dissemination of information about and from young people. Policy decisions at local and national levels should embrace a concern for realistic information giving and an improvement in the general communications that take place across the generations. However, this has to mean real action; not just action on superficial appearances, P.R. and 'fine words'. Resources, human and material are required here. That means money and it also means the political will to carry this through.

REFERENCES:
ASTLEY, J. Present Imperfect: Future Tense? *Sociology Review* Vol.1 No.1, 1991.
BANKS, M. *et al, Careers and Identities*. Open University Press, 1991.
BYNNER, J. Coping with Transition: ESRC's new 16-19 Initiative. *Youth and Policy* No.22, 1987.
CLARKE, J. and SAUNDERS, C. Who are you and so what? *Sociology Review* Vol.1 No.1, 1991
MACDONALD, R. and COFFIELD, F. *Risky Business? Youth and the Enterprise Culture*. Falmer Press, 1991.

Printed in the United Kingdom
by Lightning Source UK Ltd.
107784UKS00001B/23

9 780955 183409